TRENDS PERFECT

BEDROOM and BATHROOM

TRENDS PERFECT
BEDROOM
and BATHROOM

Sunset

Sunset

Sunset Books
80 Willow Road
Menlo Park, CA 94025

www.sunset.com

Trends *Perfect Bedroom and Bathroom* is produced in association with:
Trends Publishing International, Auckland, New Zealand.
www.trendsideas.com

Publisher: David Johnson
Editorial Director: Paul Taylor
Trends Home Series Editor: Rachel Galyer
Associate Editor: Kelli Robson
Production Director: Louise Messer
Editorial Administrator: Kate Ballinger

Chief Executive Officer: John Owen
President: Terry Newell
Publisher: Lynn Humphries
Managing Editor: Angela Handley
Design Manager: Helen Perks
Editorial Coordinator: Kiren Thandi
Production Manager: Caroline Webber
Production Coordinator: James Blackman
Sales Manager: Emily Jahn
Vice President International Sales: Stuart Laurence
Series Design Concept: John Bull
Project Designer: Lena Lowe
Text: Julia Richardson

ISBN 0-376-00178-X

Color reproduction by SC (Sang Choy) International Pte Ltd
Printed by SNP Leefung
Printed in China

A Weldon Owen Production

Cover photography
Back cover TOP LEFT Architect: Chris Ralston; Photographer: Anton Curley.
TOP RIGHT Consultant: Jeff Tan, Unique Kitchen Fusion; Photographer: Peter Mealin.
BOTTOM LEFT Hedgpeth Architects; Photographer: Tim Maloney. BOTTOM RIGHT Designer: Hardy
Interiors; Photographer: Simon Kenny.
Spine Designer: Lynn Orloff-Wilson; Photographer: Simon Kenny.
Front cover TOP LEFT Architect: Gerard Murtagh; Photographer: David Sandison TOP RIGHT Kitchen
Designer: Kitchens by Design; Photographer: Gérald Lopez BOTTOM LEFT Architect: John Chaplin;
Kitchen Designer: Ingrid Geldof; Photographer: Doc Ross. BOTTOM RIGHT Architect: Diana Meckfessel;
Photographer: Tim Maloney.

CONTENTS

INTRODUCTION

Much is expected of bedrooms and bathrooms in the modern home. They must do duty as the rooms in which we sleep and bathe, of course, but they also have the potential to be our personal safe havens, to be our refuge not only from the pressure and pace of the world outside, but also from the activity within the household. They are, in fact, the ultimate sanctuary.

① This private courtyard's solid walls and the use of limestone for the bathroom tiles and external pavers ensure that the two zones read as a single space, even when the glass doors are closed.

①

② Thanks to changing floor levels and overlapping vertical structures, such as sliding glass doors and solid masonry walls, this bedroom enjoys a relaxing sense of space but still feels cozy and contained.

②

SAFE HAVENS

It's decades now since trend-spotter Faith Popcorn coined the term "cocooning." She used it to put a name to the modern desire to hide away in a home environment that feels warm, secure, personal, special.

Since then, the world has only grown more alienating. Business is even more computer-driven. Leisure time is increasingly technology-based. Personal relationships are frequently handled screen-to-screen rather than face-to-face. And so we snuggle deeper into our cocoons, looking for tangible, sensual comforts, seeking physical and psychological distance from the troubles beyond the front door.

Some of this cocooning takes place in living rooms, dining rooms and kitchens in the company of family and friends, but the rooms that offer the deepest sense of sanctuary are the intimate spaces of the bedroom and bathroom. It's here that we come to replenish ourselves by cleansing our bodies and resting our minds.

The roles of the bedroom and the bathroom now extend beyond their primary functions. We don't occupy those spaces only when we want to sleep or bathe; we go there when we want to relax, away from the hustle of the work day and the bustle of a busy household. In the contemporary home, the bedroom and bathroom operate as private retreats, a change in perspective that has had a significant impact on how those spaces are designed and decorated.

Indeed, it has impacted on the floorplan of the modern home. Bedroom sizes, whittled away by pragmatists who reasoned that the act of sleeping didn't require space for much more than the bed itself, are now on the increase. Bathrooms are also growing larger and more plentiful, by virtue of the prevalence of master bathrooms and guest bathrooms, sometimes one for every bedroom in the house.

But floor area alone is no guarantee that either bedroom or bathroom will become the personal havens we seem to want them to be. The key is to stop thinking of these rooms as purely functional rooms and to start thinking of them as living spaces.

The bedroom is obviously the space in which you sleep and dress, but it could also be the place where you sit and eat breakfast, quietly, privately each morning. In a large bedroom that might suggest something as wonderful as a petite breakfast balcony, but in a small one it might simply mean finding space in a corner for a comfortable armchair and a little side table. Or you might enjoy the solitary indulgence of watching classic black-and-white movies while the rest of the household gathers around the television to watch football in the evening. The spacious bedroom might incorporate a separate sitting area, complete with a handsome cabinet that can be opened up to reveal audiovisual equipment and an extensive video library. The petite bedroom, meanwhile, might mount a small television on a wall-bracket and keep DVDs under the bedside table in a wicker basket.

Unlike their predecessors, modern bathrooms aim to create livable environments, complete with fresh air, plentiful natural light and even appealing views. And those bright and breezy spaces are being used not just for the morning shower, but for long afternoons of pampering or deeply soothing evenings in a long, hot bath. With such a bathroom in place, those reviving

❶

❶ This suite follows the contemporary trend toward vast parents' retreats containing a number of different types of living spaces. In this instance, a full-size living room supplements the bedroom.

❷ Building a house from scratch provides the opportunity to think strategically about the orientation of the bedroom. Here, the master bedroom looks toward seemingly limitless mountain views, maximizes intake of natural light through extensive glazing and uses a small panel of glass louvers to catch the skimming cross-breezes of the site.

❸ In an early 20th-century apartment building, the vista of city lights is the bathroom's undisputed focal point. Exposed plumbing and industrial wall lights emphasize the hard-edged urban glamour of the space.

❷

❸

soaks and luscious beauty treatments might be just as pleasurable — perhaps more so — than an afternoon at the movies or a night out at an expensive restaurant.

Creative thinking unlocks the potential of these spaces, transforming clinical bathrooms and indifferent bedrooms into sensual safe havens. For one person, that might mean setting up a library in the bedroom. For another it could mean an open fireplace at the foot of the bathtub. But it certainly doesn't have to be as conceptually extravagant as that. A yoga mat costs next to nothing, for example, but storing it in the bedroom and organizing the furniture so that there is always room to spread it out and exercise could improve your physical and mental health. A can of paint takes only hours to apply to the walls of a bedroom, but if it's just the right shade of mountain-top blue or tiger lily pink, it could mean that you wake each morning in a calm or in an energized frame of mind. And a little wire shelf mounted on the wall beside the bath and lined with bath salts and scented candles could make the difference between a night of restless fidgeting and a sound, eight-hour sleep.

The exercise of designing and decorating a bedroom or a bathroom is an opportunity to remember just what it is that gives you a feeling of peace and contentment — and to find ways to make those feelings part of your everyday experience.

❶ It's not only the size of the space that makes this master bedroom feel so indulgent, it's also the styling. Fully upholstered armchairs and lounges, an upholstered bed and plush carpeting make this a very well-padded cocoon indeed.

❶

❷ A bathroom will only have those desirable mood-enhancing qualities if it first fulfills its functional role. Good lighting and adequate storage are essential. Without them, even the most extravagant space fails to please.   ❷

1

BEDROOMS

The bedroom that provides us with a sound sleep is doing important work, fostering our physical and mental health. Yet when styled as a living space as well as a sleeping space, it can do even more. This is our private domain, the home within a home, in which we can escape the demands of family and work.

PERFECT BEDROOMS

The idea that we might spend our leisure time in the bedroom has changed the way we design and decorate this space. At one extreme, it has given rise to the concepts of the master suite and even the parents' retreat, collections of rooms that might, for example, include a sleeping space, an exercise area, a study, a separate dressing room. At the other extreme are teenagers and young adults who seek to personalize their family bedrooms, dorm rooms or first apartments simply by means of a distinctive choice of bed linen.

One of these ideas requires healthy finances and an abundance of space; the other needs little more than a bed and a few dollars. Yet they both show a desire for personal territory, even within a comfortable and sociable household.

We need our sleep. Shift workers, international travelers, overworked executives, students, new parents and insomniacs know that without adequate sleep we can be forgetful, distracted and overly emotional at the very least. We may even suffer from poor health and depression. It's not overstating the case to say that we have a responsibility to ourselves and to those around us to try to make this a space conducive to restorative sleep.

A good bed is probably the single most important factor. Without a suitably supportive mattress, your sleep will be restless and you may even wake stiff and sore as well as tired.

PREVIOUS PAGES A grand suite might have the luxury of space in which to install a well-furnished sitting area, but even a single armchair can expand the potential of the bedroom, making it a place to sit and read or listen to music as well as a place in which to sleep and dress.

❶ To look out at the ocean's horizon is to gaze on spirit-lifting wilderness. Not every bedroom has the gift of a sea view, but even in the absence of such a panorama, the gentle touch of morning sun can bring a great sense of calm to the space.

❶

❷ ❸
❹ ❺

❷ The tranquility of the garden view is brought inside this bedroom by the framed print and the serene choice of color.

❸ Achieving success in bedroom decorating means being clear and honest about what sorts of textures and colors you find most appealing. For some, it may be the freshness of white walls and floods of daylight. Others may prefer the moody warmth of bare wood and earthy browns.

❹ Extensive glazing takes advantage of the rolling country vista, but broad wooden shutters mean that the room can be shut tight against unwanted daylight.

❺ The patch of floorspace provided by a bay window is just the spot for a sitting area.

❶

❷

❶ A thoughtful combination of light fittings gives this bedroom a great deal of flexibility. The ceiling and wall lights play a functional role, the former providing general illumination for tasks such as dressing or changing the bed linen, the latter providing focused light for reading. If there isn't a need for strong illumination, the floor lamp can be used to give the room a gentle glow.

Budgets play a part, of course, but it is important to choose the best-quality mattress you can afford and to replace that mattress when it begins to show signs of wear.

It is also necessary to have as much control as possible over both light and sound. If bright streetlights or car headlights are likely to wake you or if you have a need to sleep beyond sunrise, then you must install blinds or curtains capable of blocking out that unwanted light. Similarly, if noise is likely to disrupt your sleep, do what you can to minimize the problem. This could mean relocating the bedroom to a room further from the street or at a greater distance from a noisy family living area. It could mean installing double-glazed windows or exterior shutters that can be closed tight against external noise. Or it could mean putting in place a strategy to mask an inescapable noise: leaving the radio on over night, for example,

❷ When both the glass doors and the folding wooden doors are closed, this bedroom is shut fast against light and noise. When the glass doors are slid back and the doors set with louvers open, the space can enjoy cooling night breezes.

❸ Panels of tinted louvers play a striking decorative role, as well as encouraging air flow around the room.

❸

❶ Built as an addition to a 1950s beach house, this bedroom embraces the simple structures of the vacation house. Two walls are made from horizontal panels of poly-carbonate. The other two use wood paneling, reflecting the vintage of the original house.

❶

❷ Sliding doors on two sides can be retracted to fully expose this bedroom to an adjacent courtyard. Such transparency may not be to everyone's taste, but it allows the room to reach out into open space, enjoying the light, the breezes and the sounds of the outdoors.

❷

or buying a sound unit that plays audio of waves lapping on the shore or wind whispering in the treetops.

We need our sleep, but we also need some active time alone. The trend toward open-plan living has energized the modern home, but it has also influenced us to think of our bedrooms as living spaces as well as sleeping spaces. The bedroom is a private domain, a place in which we might read, do some simple exercises, meditate, perhaps quietly greet the morning with a cup of coffee or see out the day with a glass of herbal tea. Think of these possibilities when devising the floorplan of the bedroom, and look at ways of making space for these activities, even in a small room.

It's useful to think of the bedroom as an emotional space, as well as a functional one. Having found ways of making this room meet your needs in a functional way, it is time to consider how it might engage you or connect with you in a personal and intimate way.

For some, this might be a matter of aesthetics. It could mean giving this room the liberatingly clean lines of fresh-faced minimalism. For others it could purely be a matter of color, a decision to rise each morning in a room of dewy green, to relax at the end of the day enveloped by Tahiti pink or to sink into sleep surrounded by clouds of lavender. For still others it might be a more literal affair. The bedroom could become a narrative of past travels, a four-walled family album of photographs or a childhood dream of romance.

The bedroom that makes space for living as well as sleeping becomes a home within a home for the occupant. The bedroom that looks and feels like a deeply personal creation, that touches the emotions and delights the senses, becomes the satisfying sanctuary of which we all dream.

2

MODERN BEDROOMS

The contemporary bedroom is a room for living, not just for sleeping. Increasingly, the master bedroom in a modern home includes a dressing room, home office, home gym or sitting area. It is also a sensory space, using light, sound, texture and color to create an indulgent and intimate retreat.

MODERN BEDROOMS

All the knowledge of modern architecture is invested in the design of the contemporary bedroom. Square rooms, centrally located beds and demurely draped windows are no longer the standard. In their place are fresh ideas about floorplans that incorporate living and working spaces, windows that let in the light and permit the room to connect with the world outside and materials that ensure comfort.

Contemporary bedrooms often section off areas of the room for different purposes: a walk-in wardrobe, a study, a small sitting area, even a quiet-time play area for young children within a parents' room, for example. Sometimes the demarcation can be achieved through furniture arrangements. At other times, more substantial methods are required for the room to function well. It might be necessary to use a free-standing decorative screen to separate a home office from

PREVIOUS PAGES In an effort to gain floor-space and take advantage of natural sources of light and ventilation, the modern bedroom often comes perilously close to compromising its privacy. Design elements such as split floor levels and features such as etched glass doors make it possible to have it all.

❶ Tucked into a pocket of roof space, this bedroom offers seclusion. It has been necessary, however, to employ some creative solutions to make the oddly shaped space appealing and to incorporate an office area. Custom cabinetry makes the most of the shortened volumes under the sloping eaves.

the sleeping area so that the clutter of work does not spill into the tranquil surrounds of the bed. Blade walls that stop short of the ceiling are a common tool, frequently used to define a dressing area. Perhaps the most familiar arrangement sees the blade wall serving as a headboard (often upholstered with silk or linen or painted in a feature color) while also functioning as one wall of a galley-style walk-in wardrobe.

The trend toward using the bedroom as a living space as well as a sleeping space has been matched by design strategies that make the room more pleasant to inhabit during daylight hours. These include large expanses of glazing that offer views, serve as a source of natural light and can also be used to promote refreshing cross breezes. The need for privacy in urban areas sometimes sees these windows positioned above head height or installed as vertical or horizontal slits that obscure views of the interior from outside.

The contemporary bedroom demonstrates that every element — from the rug on the floor to the fabric of the pillow case — has a capacity to delight the senses. Thick rugs and carpets, textured wallpapers and paint finishes, plush upholstery fabrics and bed linen are all used to make the bedroom a tactile space as well as a visual one, and set the bedroom apart as a place of complete sanctuary.

❶ Bedrooms in tropical areas must do whatever is possible to encourage a cross-flow of cooling breezes, but the windows and other openings required can leave the space feeling empty and exposed. Here, a deep shade of terra cotta makes an airy room feel welcoming.

❶

❷ This master suite is set apart from the main body of the house, accessible only by a walkway lined with polycarbonate sheeting and glass louvers. The breeze-swept journey away from the living areas and into the bedroom creates an almost tangible feeling of retreat. ❷

❶ Set against snowy, mountainous country-side, this bedroom combines traditional building materials with a modern floorplan. The solid wooden walls, a full 12 inches (30 cm) thick, and the wooden cladding on the barrel-vaulted ceiling make this room look and feel warm and cozy. The slate-covered floor plays an important role in the thermal functioning of the entire house, absorbing and holding heat when the sun is shining, then releasing it when the temperature drops. The extensive glazing helps to draw in the sunshine and offers a staggering mountain view. Built-in furnishings and a freestanding fireplace have been positioned so that they don't intrude on the view from the bed itself.

❷ The majority of modern interiors are constructed in a streamlined fashion, without the detail of cornices, decorative skirting boards or elaborate lights. In this bedroom, a shaggy bedspread and a matching cushion introduce a tactile element to a space that might otherwise have been texturally bland.

❸ Built-in cabinetry and separate walk-in dressing rooms are both popular ways of keeping clutter out of sight. In this bedroom, the pared-back look is enhanced by a simple platform bed and chic but plain bed linen.

❶

❷

❸

❶

❶ This bedroom is an example of how freestanding walls can be used to create zones within a larger space. In this case, a half-height wall makes a long, narrow room more manageable, separating the sleeping area from the dressing area to the rear.

❷ The floor area of this dressing room is in fact quite limited and, had it been built as an independent room, it would have felt cramped. As it is, it gives the impression of being a generous space, well endowed with natural light and benefiting from the sense of scale created by the high, pitched ceiling. The strategy of building the two wardrobes as twin built-in storage units in opposite corners has created a nook overlooked by a window. Currently the counter serves as a dressing table, but it could also be used as desk space in a compact home office.

❷

① A Japanese influence is at play in this warm bedroom. Customized cabinetry makes the room functional without being cluttered. A window box pushes out into the garden, blurring the distinction between the interior and the exterior. Dark shades of nut brown, bronze and amber form an organic but sophisticated palette that helps to relate the bedroom to the greenery beyond the glass.

② This vivacious bedroom subverts its inherently clean lines with objects that are curvaceous and richly idiosyncratic. The room itself is quite simple and streamlined, as are the bed and bedside tables. A whimsical chandelier light fitting and a voluptuous armchair introduce the eclecticism that is characteristic of 21st-century interiors.

❶

❷

❸

❶ This airy, light-hearted bedroom incorporates an internal balcony, accessible through wood-framed glass doors. The balcony overlooks the dining room on the floor below. The structure gives the bedroom an extra sense of space and volume and allows it to take advantage of the light coming in through windows right around the house.

❷ One wall was painted violet to maximize the impact of the room's only decorative touch, a painting in gray tones.

❸ The "walls" in this bedroom are formed by thick columns, spanned by counter-height cabinets. The colonnade effect helps to make this space feel enclosed and intimate despite the absence of solid walls.

❹ Space was found for two extra bedrooms in this family house by excavating below ground level. An olive-tinged gray paint color enhances the feeling of seclusion.

❹

❶

❶ By virtue of some tall panels of glazing, this bedroom takes as its territory the adjacent courtyard. Visually, the connection is always there, but it's also easy to slide back one of those panels, allowing the sounds and the breezes of the outdoors to enter the room, or coaxing the room's occupants out into open space. Full eaves shade the courtyard and keep the bedroom cool in this hot desert environment.

❷ In this master suite, an angled, three-quarter-height blade wall separates the bedroom from the bathroom. The looseness of the structure reflects the commitment to open-plan living throughout the house. The depth of the wall makes it possible for it to serve as storage space on the bedroom side and house the necessary plumbing and electrical cables on the bathroom side.

❷

NOSTALGIC BEDROOMS

An antique sleigh bed, an original mantelpiece or an heirloom patchwork quilt: the elements of the nostalgic bedroom connect us to other people, places and times. Such pieces bring with them a deeply comforting sense of history and humanity, setting the scene for a warm and welcoming bedroom.

NOSTALGIC BEDROOMS

Bedrooms that draw on a nostalgia for times past are, in a surprising way, perfect for contemporary lifestyles. In a world where human interactions are often replaced by technology, it seems we are reaching out, quite literally with our fingertips, to touch surfaces once owned, used and loved by other hands at other times in history. Designers of brand-new homes and apartments are scouring antique dealerships and salvage yards for pre-used wood, bricks, hearth stones, windows and doors that will bring a sense of age and continuity into the most modern of spaces.

At home, in the bedroom, the need is being met by antique beds and bed linen, old family photographs and sentimental relics of childhood, such as old teddy bears or tennis rackets — in short, by anything that carries with it some kind of story, be it personal or cultural.

PREVIOUS PAGES Nostalgic bedrooms don't have to be dark or forbidding. In both these rooms, a rich egg-yolk yellow radiates with a warmth that makes the traditional furnishings seem welcoming rather than austere.

❶ Original brass beds in good condition might be hard to come by these days, but quality reproductions are available. Brass beds have a less formal air than some of the ornate wooden beds of similar vintage, and are well suited to a relaxed space.

The nostalgic bedroom is wide open to interpretation. For some, it means the complete, period-perfect package: from historic wallpaper to ornate traditional window dressings to four-poster beds topped with heavily decorative canopies. Of course, this depth of authenticity can only be played out in a house of the appropriate architectural style.

The golden glow of nostalgia can also be summoned up with a single element, but that element must be able to serve as the focal point of the room. Beds tend to be the centerpiece of the bedroom by default, so the strongest and safest strategy is to choose a bed with a history — something handmade and rustic found in an old farmhouse, for example, or a bewitchingly sinuous iron bed picked up in a French market. Other bedroom furnishings — for instance, a set of old wooden lockers serving as a wardrobe, an age-worn kilim on the floor or a handmade box being used as a bedside table — can also convey a warm and sentimental sense of history. So, too, can an artful display of family memorabilia, be it a set of photos from childhood vacations at the beach, a model of the lighthouse once occupied by a great-grandfather or a series of oars used as part of a long-standing family sporting tradition.

❶ An antique bed is not an essential element of the nostalgic bedroom. Here, patterned wallpaper and bed linen create a richly evocative environment around a simple furniture ensemble.

❶

❷

❷ Modern mattress sizes sometimes don't correlate with the proportions of vintage beds. A custom-made mattress was ordered for this bed so that it can do double duty as a day bed and a guest bed.

❸ A decadent use of shimmering silk taffeta gives the traditional look a sophisticated edge.   ❸

❶

❷

❶ Even period devotees sometimes relegate canopies to a purely decorative role, but they can be used to great effect in the nostalgically styled modern bedroom. For example, in a large master bedroom that includes a sitting area for book reading or television watching, a canopy can be used to block out unwanted light when one partner chooses to retire to bed. Here, the rooftop of fabric counters the extreme height of the ceiling, making this a more intimate space.

❷ Brass beds, hand-stitched quilts and an exuberant collision of color and pattern are characteristic of the traditional country look. In this instance, sisal flooring has been used to give this reasonably refined space an appropriately rugged, rustic base.

③

④

③ Some nostalgic bedrooms are faithful reproductions of the originals, as is the case here. The owners of this late Victorian villa were so committed to the refurbishment that they delved into the archives of the local historical society to find a pattern from which they could copy this lacy canopy.

④ The idiosyncracies of this room were impossible to ignore. The curved ceiling and unusually deep wall niches dictated the style of the bedroom's furnishings, bed linen and window dressings.

There are two ways of creating the perfect nostalgic bedroom. One is to capitalize on the strong contrast between an old piece and other contemporary furnishings. Imagine, for example, a glorious antique sleigh bed, gleaming like aged burnished leather, flanked by two perfectly white, square-cut storage cubes serving as bedside tables and topped with fine-boned aluminum reading lights.

The other approach is to select furnishings that somehow sympathize with the age of the centerpiece. They can either exhibit a time-worn, textural finish or make a reference to the period through color or pattern. Bleached wooden floorboards, for instance, would be a charming base for an old iron day bed, and drapes that reproduce vintage patterns could enhance the presence of an old wardrobe.

❶ A brass bed sets the tone for this nostalgic space, but the room's most appealing feature is undoubtedly its collection of framed family photographs. The frames have been aligned so that the lower edge of the group forms a single straight line: this treatment gives the collection decorative strength despite the variety of individual frames.

❷ An original marble fireplace is something to cherish. Here, a dark wood-framed mirror has a commanding presence and the lack of clutter updates the look.

❸ A scallop-edged Marcella quilt, a traditional French bed dressing, is well suited to this arrangement of antiques.

❶ This bedroom of thoroughly authentic appearance has in fact been put together with brand-new pieces of furniture, styled to have the look of classic English antiques. Although some devotees prefer to purchase originals, reproduction furnishings have their advantages. For example, it is far easier to buy a complete set of newly made furniture than it is to put together a collection through numerous visits to antique dealerships and auction houses. Another advantage is that reproduction pieces usually accommodate contemporary standards, such as mattress sizes. Indeed, the very best reproductions are of a quality that will see them become heirlooms in their own right.

❷ The swirling fabric of the canopy and the painterly feature cushion introduce an angelic quality to this bedroom, a sense of whimsy not always present in traditional spaces.

❸ Reproduction furniture pieces have been used to recreate a nostalgic decor in this modern bedroom. Their style makes an important contribution to the character of the room, but the most influential feature is the ornate canopy.

CLASSIC BEDROOMS

There are no bright lights or vibrant colors here, no attention-grabbing patterns or pace-setting trends. The classic bedroom — muted in tone, mellow in style — is an oasis of calm. It promises timeless beauty and a blissful absence of stimuli, qualities that assure its success as a peaceful retreat.

CLASSIC BEDROOMS

No other bedroom is quite as tranquil as the classically styled space. It is a world unto itself, a safe harbor of serenity, that is free of emotional color cues or fashion-charged features and finishes.

In theory at least, the basic elements of the classic bedroom — such as wall treatments, flooring, furniture and window dressings — should last well over a decade. The challenge is to select fittings and finishes that will endure. The solution is to look for pieces, materials and colors that are fashion-neutral and the best quality possible within your budget.

A good carpet, preferably wool or wool blend, in a neutral tone is a sensible choice. It will provide a suitably subtle base for the room and promises all the comforting visual and tactile warmth of soft flooring. Shades of white, cream and beige are the obvious choices, but remember that, as our understanding of color has grown more sophisticated, the concept of neutral shades has expanded to include stronger hues, such as charcoal and eggplant.

PREVIOUS PAGES A restrained palette, free of contrasts and accents that might distract the eye, helps to achieve a sense of calm in the classically styled bedroom.

❶ Soft surfaces, including the plush carpet and upholstered headboard, in combination with a low ceiling, mute the acoustics of this room, ensuring that it is as easy on the ear as it is on the eye.

❶ Upholstered walls cosset this room in a real and tactile way. The textured surface of the fabric introduces a level of interest to the room without intruding on the serenity achieved by an essentially monochromatic color scheme. The treatment also serves as an acoustic buffer, making this a blissfully quiet retreat.

❷ The check of the fabric used on the wing chair makes a connection with the grid-like paving of the courtyard outside the French doors.

❶

❷

Wooden floorboards are the most popular alternative to carpet and are a must for some homeowners. It's important to appreciate that different species of wood have different hues and so must be considered as part of the overall palette of the room. Floorboards can create a noisy environment, which isn't always a very desirable outcome in a bedroom, particularly in the low-key surrounds of the classically styled space. Some floor rugs will help to keep the noise down. Position them by the bed so that you find a soft surface underfoot as you step out of bed in the morning.

❶ Simple lines tend to endure beyond the fashions of the day. Here, they are evident not only in the design of the bed and the bedside tables, but also in the appealingly plain venetian blind that serves as a window dressing for an enormous expanse of glazing.

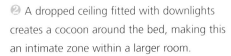

 A dropped ceiling fitted with downlights creates a cocoon around the bed, making this an intimate zone within a larger room.

❸ This master bedroom is in a 1920s-era house built in the French Revival style. New additions, such as the custom-built bed with its tall pearwood veneer headboard, imitate the lean lines of the building's original style, visible in the decorative paneling of the walls. This deft and sympathetic combination of old and new creates an environment that feels fresh and modern, yet gracefully timeless.

❹ Dark, glossy floorboards have a handsome look, but they also form a reflective surface that can make for a noisy environment. The floor rug under the bed muffles the acoustics of the room.

❶ Custom-built wardrobes feature glass-paneled door fronts backed by gathered fabric — a suitable choice for this softly styled space. The sympathetic design of the built-in storage helps to minimize its visual impact.

❶

❷ Layers of soft furnishings can make for a sumptuous environment, but the strategy must be handled with care if it is to succeed in the subdued surrounds of the classic bedroom. A multitude of patterns might look warm and welcoming in a nostalgic room, but in the classic bedroom it can be out of place. The solution here was to use a single print, with solid colors as support.

❷

Seek out neutral tones for the walls, too, but avoid the stronger tones suggested for carpets as they will be too overwhelming when wrapped around all four sides of the room. Also avoid trendy paint finishes like rag washing and sueded looks: they will show their age before long. Wallpapers are another possibility, as long as you opt for timeless patterns such as fine stripes or very subtle florals.

Look for clean lines in window treatments, favoring simple drops of fabric or smart roman blinds over the frills of fancy drapes. The shapes and colors of furnishings, too, should be as plain as possible, but as sumptuous as you please in terms of texture and comfort. Appealing as it might be to introduce a personal decorative note, it's important to realize that even the tiniest details — the selection of painted ceramic or cut-glass drawer pulls on a chest of drawers, for example — will eventually date the piece and ultimately undermine the sublime composure of the classic bedroom.

❶ Storage is a key issue in classic bedrooms — after all, there is little point designing and decorating a room to be a sublimely peaceful place if it is permanently strewed with discarded clothes. The redesign of this suite included the installation of a blade wall, which serves as a headboard with built-in storage, and creates a wardrobe to the rear.

❷ A palette of weathered tones and finishes was intentionally put together to make this coastal home feel not only calm, but casual.

❶

❷

❶ ❷

❶ Housed inside an old beach hut, this bedroom makes the most of its architectural character. While the weatherboard cladding and the steel trussing beneath the ceiling are original, the floor of waxed concrete is new. The floor treatment maintains the inherent unpretentiousness of the space, a quality that lends the room all the casual charm of a childhood vacation house.

❷ This bedroom sits inside a simple, seaside house, constructed entirely of wood. The wooden surfaces of the ceiling and walls bestow upon the room a lightly nostalgic mood, but the white-wash treatment given to the floorboards contributes a fresh and modern look. The net effect is a bedroom with timeless appeal.

③

④

③ While undeniably soothing in character, monochromatic color schemes can be unimpressive. Here, the approach is made more sophisticated through the use of textures. The bed linen was chosen because of its woven pattern and the ribbed sisal flooring for its agreeably rugged texture. The centerpiece of the room is a mirror, framed with an antique Oriental wedding sash.

④ The challenge here was to have a room that expressed some of the drama of the house's contemporary architecture, while maintaining the composure of a classically styled bedroom. Instead of the predictable shades of beige, this room combines olive, gray, mauve and khaki with an unusually dark red for an essentially neutral palette that embodies an element of confidence.

5

CHARACTER BEDROOMS

A bedroom is a private space. It doesn't have to service the needs
of the household at large or accommodate guests. Like no other
room in the house, it is yours to do with as you please. You can
choose to create the atmosphere of a tropical oasis, decorate it
with personal keepsakes or fashion it as a diva's dressing room.

FANTASY BEDROOMS

The decoration of a bedroom doesn't require the same focus on function and efficiency as the design of a bathroom or a kitchen. Naturally, a bedroom must provide a place to sleep and some space to store clothes, but beyond that it is open to interpretation. Why shouldn't the bedroom be the realization of personal taste and vision, the physical embodiment of the long-held dreams of its occupants?

It is possible that the room itself will set the tone for this fantasy: imagine tucking a bedroom inside the turrets of a Victorian mansion or turning an old wooden shed in the backyard into a teenager's apartment.

In most cases, though, the furniture will establish the desired mood. Usually a single, distinctive piece is all that's required. Start with an oversized, Southeast Asian, carved wooden canopy bed, bedecked with a mosquito net, and the room immediately takes on a tropical air. Or install a silvery dressing

PREVIOUS PAGES The gilt and glamour of a five-star resort may be the ultimate fantasy bedroom for some. A room of such lavish proportions certainly lends itself to this indulgence, but the same sort of atmosphere can be recreated in more modest spaces by using opulent colors and textures.

❶ This glittering room is tailor-made for a 21st-century Joan Crawford or Bette Davis. The silver-leaf finish and elegant styling of the contemporary dressing table recall the high glamour of Hollywood's Golden Years, a mood enhanced by shimmering textiles and plush floor coverings.

①

❶ From the window dressings to the layers of pillows and cushions, this room has a lot of frills and flourishes. It's an undeniably sugary look, yet it avoids being too sweet by virtue of its predominantly white color scheme, anchored by an earthy natural floor covering.

②

table topped with a winged vanity mirror to introduce a note of old-time Hollywood glamour.

When dressing a room comprehensively according to a theme, it's important to avoid looking gimmicky. In most cases, the best approach is to allow a single character piece to serve as a focal point and to furnish the rest of the bedroom in a more restrained style. The exception is when the entire house is influenced by a particular style. For example, in a converted warehouse filled with reinvented industrial furnishings, it makes sense to use an old tool cabinet for a wardrobe, a piece of salvaged metal for a headboard and to hang oversized cogs on the bedroom wall for decoration. Or, if Moroccan architecture is your inspiration from front gate to roof garden, follow through with a window seat covered in vibrant cushions, a candelabrum hanging from the ceiling and copper urns filled with fragrant flowers set on bedside tables.

❷ This particular flight of fancy includes a meditative interior garden, complete with water feature. Together with a soaring ceiling, these unusual elements produce a temple-like atmosphere. The wooden walkway crosses a shallow pool to give access to a similarly contemplative sitting area.

❸ Taking its inspiration from traditional Balinese architecture, this bedroom was purpose-built as an independent pavilion, linked to the main part of the house by a covered walkway. Indonesian furnishings, including the sumptuous canopied four-poster bed, invest the room with authenticity.   ❸

❶ With its model airplane, rustic antique bed and window dressings designed to appear medieval, this bedroom expresses some diverse influences. A consistency of tone and a common sense of age and patina successfully link these elements.

❶

❷ A rendered wall, which serves as a headboard and incorporates storage niches, is a suitably blank canvas for the display of curios and keepsakes, from hand-me-down suitcases to favorite books. A mannequin displays a military jacket that would otherwise be tucked out of sight in a closet. The overall effect is delightfully rich.

❷

SOUVENIR BEDROOMS

Most of us have collected a considerable treasury of personal memorabilia. There might be a suitcase full of boarding passes, tram tickets and well-worn maps from a grand tour of the world. There might be an attic crammed with sailing trophies, newspaper clippings of yachts crossing the finishing line, a father's sailing cap, hand-built model boats and so on. There might be tea chests brimming with old photographs, a faded street sign, handwritten letters, a watercolor of a little old cottage hung with wisteria — all reminders of childhood visits to a much-loved grandparent's home.

Sometimes it's not possible to integrate these deeply affecting personal mementos into the house at large. The sentimentality of an old street sign would look out of place in a stainless steel kitchen. Weathered maps, even framed, would look odd beside collectable contemporary lithographs in the living room.

The bedroom, though, is more at ease with such intimacy. Indeed, bedrooms that are decorated with such souvenirs can be immensely pleasurable spaces to inhabit. They are so entirely different from any other space you might occupy throughout the day — so personal, warm and welcoming — that they are surprisingly effective at providing the cocoon of comfort so desired in the contemporary home.

If you do opt for a nostalgic mood, don't let your bedroom become a museum space. Design and furnish the room as a functioning bedroom first, and then use your souvenirs to color the space. Remember, too, that the sheer number and diversity of your keepsakes will provide more than enough visual interest, so paint colors, fabrics and furnishings should be relatively subdued.

EASTERN BEDROOMS

Eastern aesthetics have had a lasting impact on Western ideas about design and decorating. While the idea of using Oriental looks in a contemporary home might once have been seen as faddish, it is now commonplace.

Of course, the term "Eastern" represents a diversity of styles and traditions, from the richness of North Africa and the Middle East to the opulence of India and the impeccable discipline of Japanese design. The Eastern-influenced bedroom might take its cue from any one of these, but it should avoid the aesthetic muddle of mixing and matching across cultures.

Furniture, accessories and textiles from India, Japan, Vietnam, Thailand, Indonesia and some of the Arab and North African nations are readily available in the West, not only in specialty stores, but often on the shop floors of the major chain stores and department stores. As a result, it's a relatively easy matter to comprehensively dress an Eastern-styled bedroom, from the rugs on the floor to the fabric of the drapes and the lighting.

At first glance it might look as though the dramatic wall hanging is the only Japanese element of this space. In fact this bedroom was designed as a contemporary reflection of traditional Japanese style. The calming colors and uncluttered floorplan convey a distinctive Zen-like style. More specific references are made in details such as the windows, where horizontal paneling recalls the form of Japanese shoji screens.

❶

The alternative is to feature a single scene-stealing piece and then furnish the rest of the room with items of a less striking nature. This balance is crucial: the impact of a single, dramatic character piece will be diminished if it has to compete for attention with a second or third personality piece.

At the same time, all of your furnishings should share some common ground in terms of color, shape or finish. For example, use rustic cupboards from central Asia with carved and painted doors for clothes storage, and offset them with simple wooden furnishings, lightly finished with a tinted wood wash. Or use a sliding Japanese shoji screen as a partition between the sleeping area and the master bathroom, and introduce the characteristic Japanese red as a paint color on the walls or as scatter cushions.

❶ Sympathetic tones of charcoal gray and chocolate brown extend the influence of an antique Japanese chest positioned at the foot of the bed. The colors infuse the space with a subtle but handsome Oriental undertone.

❷ Sleek, low-line furnishings, a relatively sparse floorplan and a clear connection with the natural world via tall panels of glazing play out a Japanese style without falling into cultural pastiche. A set of prints featuring Japanese calligraphy highlights the reasonably low-key theme.

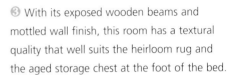

②

③ With its exposed wooden beams and mottled wall finish, this room has a textural quality that well suits the heirloom rug and the aged storage chest at the foot of the bed.

④ The traditional aesthetics of cultures poised on the northernmost edge of Africa — places such as Tunisia and Algeria — have an alluring presence that has captured the imagination of Western designers. These large, painted doors, with their metal studs and trim, were sourced from Morocco. Their exotic appeal is enhanced by the lustrous silk bed linen and persimmon-colored walls.

③   ④

CHILDREN'S BEDROOMS

The decision to let a child take the lead in decorating his or her own bedroom has many advantages. It is a wonderful chance for that child to begin developing a sense of identity, to start recognizing the unique combination of influences and experiences that makes them different from everyone else around them. It's also a fine opportunity to award them the privilege of independence and to introduce the concept of responsibility that goes with that freedom. And it can give a child an enormous sense of accomplishment. Free rein in the child's own room may even have the effect of liberating other rooms in the household, as the bedroom becomes the child's preferred place for play and work.

It takes courage to let a child have complete say over the colors and furnishings of their room. The jungle-green walls, floors and ceiling of a little boy's dream may seem unbearably dark in a house full of gallery-white rooms. The candy pink of a little princess's parlor may be completely at odds with the red, white and blue palette of the rest of the house.

There are a number of ways in which parents can maintain some control without inhibiting the decorative desires of their children. They might, for example, give children creative licence with color (after all, walls are easily repainted when their tastes change) and encourage them to select their own bed linen, but leave the purchase of furniture, which should last for a decade or more, in the hands of the adults. Or they might present a limited number of choices, all of which are considered acceptable: This painted wooden bed or that unpainted wooden bed? This willowy green paint color or that grassy green paint color? These painted wooden shutters or those roman blinds?

❶ Awkward features that adults might find undesirable are often the quirks that delight a younger member of the family. Here, a little girl enjoys curling up in bed under the tent-like slope of a protruding staircase.

❶

❷

❷ A deep built-in storage space accommodates clothes, toys and a television. As a result, this child's bedroom can be tidied up in an instant.

❸ The wall color of this room was chosen to suit the palette of the house, but the little boy who occupies it selected his own bed.   ❸

All those high creative spirits must, however, be offset by some practicality. Children will relish the chance to choose paint colors and fabrics, but may not be quite so enthusiastic about solving storage problems — an ongoing challenge in a room in which toys, schoolbooks, sports equipment and clothes all need to be contained. If possible, devise and implement a good storage strategy before delivering the project into the hands of the children.

If siblings are to live happily side by side in a shared bedroom, they need to have some sense of personal space. Unless the children are uncommonly unified in their taste, it's probably best to leave decisions about the overall aesthetics of the room in the hands of the parents. Separate clothes storage, toy storage and work areas are desirable, but not always feasible. At the very least, try to incorporate distinctively different beds, headboards or bed linen.

❶ A custom-built work area makes this a highly functional child's room, while the clay tone of the walls and richly colored bed linen give the space a welcoming warmth.

❷ Pre-teens seem to love having all their treasures clustered around them. Shelves built into the wall alongside the bed answer that need while keeping the bulk of the toys and books off the floor.

❸ A wall of cabinetry built around a window provides an extraordinary amount of storage space, as well as creating a tempting nook in which a child could curl up to read a book or gaze out the window.

❶

❷

❶ It may look like the parlor of a little princess, but the character of this space could easily be altered with little more than a change of bed linen. The defining candy pink color is carried though in fabrics, specifically the blanket, quilt and pillowcase and the ottoman. The shell of the room — walls, flooring and joinery — is resolutely neutral, meaning that this room can easily be adapted to suit changing tastes.

❷ The minimalism of this room might well appeal to adults, but it could be a little under-stimulating to the eyes of a small child. A dashing, painted race-car bed injects a lot of personality without entirely undermining the chic austerity of the space.

③

④

③ Indulge the dreamy fantasies of a little girl by hanging a canopy over a standard, single bed. The canopy could hang from a series of hooks mounted on the ceiling or from a wall-mounted frame, as seen here. As she grows older and the decor loses its appeal, the canopy can be disassembled.

④ This smart children's bedroom might look heavily themed, but the nautical touches are easily removed simply by changing the bed linen and taking down the life rings. With their painted joinery and tailored wall lights, the bunks will retain a seaside air in keeping with the character of this vacation house.

BEDROOM LIGHTING

The modern bedroom hosts all manner of activities, from sleeping and dressing through to studying, exercising and cozying up with a favorite movie. Some of these tasks require fresh, clear daylight, others need focused electric light or a warm ambient glow. A good lighting design will ensure that all these needs are met.

BEDROOM LIGHTING

By the end of the 20th century, the need to draw natural light into the living spaces of a house or apartment was well understood by homeowners and architects alike. On a practical level, natural light reduces the need for artificial lighting and heating, both of which are big consumers of energy and have a negative impact on the environment. And on a more emotional level, the mellow warmth of sunshine makes a room feel welcoming: a space lit by the sun is far more likely to attract people to it than a space that remains dark and shadowy throughout the day.

Until recently, the bedroom was not considered a priority in this kind of sun-planning, given that it was a space primarily used at night. Increasingly, though, we are using our bedrooms as living spaces. Sometimes the bedroom has been deliberately furnished as a dual-purpose room, incorporating a home office or a parents' retreat, but even a simple bedroom can serve as a space in which to spend some nourishing personal time — meditating, reading or simply listening to music.

As a result, natural light has become a prime consideration in the bedroom. Rooms that face south in the northern hemisphere or north in the southern hemisphere will enjoy plentiful sunlight for a large part of the day. Those that face the rising sun will have the benefit of natural light in the morning, though they will most probably lose that light by

PREVIOUS PAGES The bedroom has the same need for diverse lighting options as the bathroom. At times it needs the great brilliance of the sun at full strength, pouring through well-sited windows. At other times it requires no more than the ambient light of shaded lamps, scarcely stronger than the glow of candlelight.

❶ Upright shaded lamps provide an ambient light suitable for a late evening chat with a partner, but not for the demanding task of reading. For that you need a lamp that can be angled to shine directly onto the page.

❶

❷

❷ Adjustable lamps can be pulled across to serve as reading lights or swung out of the way to provide an indirect, ambient light.

❸ This bedroom is faced with sliding panels of frosted glass instead of a solid wall, which allows the light coming in to reach right into the heart of the bedroom.   ❸

①

the afternoon. In warmer climates, rooms that face west are best avoided, as they absorb a large amount of the harsh light of the setting sun and can become intolerably hot overnight.

Of course, much time is spent in the bedroom after dark, when artificial lighting becomes a necessity. Remember that the bedroom rarely needs strong, overall illumination. Activities that do require good strong light — dressing, reading a book, applying make-up — are quite contained. Lamps and focused downlights can be used to supply the light for those tasks.

Don't make the mistake of relying on shaded table lamps for light to read by: the light will not reach the page. Instead use lamps with flexible arms that can bring light directly onto a book or newspaper. This has the extra advantage that the concentrated beam will not disrupt a sleeping partner.

① Built on a mezzanine level overlooking a uniquely styled living space, this bedroom isn't encumbered by the usual requirements for privacy, such as solid walls. The living space below is an indoor-outdoor room with banks of louvers and panels of wire mesh, ensuring a constant flow of fresh air as well as an influx of natural light. A glazed wall allows the mezzanine bedroom to take advantage of the light and air as well as sharing views of the grounds surrounding the building. Throughout the house, louver blades are made from wood rather than glass. In the bedroom, the presence of wood brings visual warmth and solidity, affording the room a much-needed intimacy.

❷ Clerestory windows bring in vast amounts of light during the day, while a series of wall-mounted uplights produce a diffuse glow after dark.

❸ A trio of windows brings some daylight into this room without compromising privacy. The neat, square shape of the windows and the graphic way in which they are aligned on the wall also gives them a decorative role.

❹ This window introduces light, air and a rooftop view to an attic bedroom. The construction of the window, including three independent blinds, maximizes its utility. For example, it would be possible to close the bi-fold windows and draw the larger blind while leaving open the slim louvers to catch evening breezes on a hot summer's night.

❶

❶ Strategically placed light fittings highlight the architectural features of this bedroom. The lights that drop from the ceiling above the bed have flexible heads that can be angled either to cast light onto the room's decorative niches, thus producing a soft, ambient light, or to provide an overhead light for reading. Concealed uplights also showcase a decorative pyramid.

❷ This simple scheme addresses all the requirements of bedroom lighting. A set of ceiling-mounted downlights provides a general, diffuse light, while a flexible wall-mounted lamp serves as a reading light. The window is hung with a sheer blind that allows an intake of natural light, even when some level of daytime privacy is required.

❷

Lights attached to the headboard or to the wall just above the bed can be similarly useful, especially when they incorporate extendable or hinged arms. These allow them to be pushed or swung out of the way when they are no longer required. Ceiling-mounted downlights can be used as reading lights, but the higher the ceiling, the more their value diminishes.

The areas around dressing tables and clothes storage should also be supplied with good, focused light. This, again, can be met by using lamps or ceiling-mounted downlights. Strip lights or downlights fitted inside the wardrobe and wired so that they switch on and off as the wardrobe door is opened and closed can be very effective and surprisingly inexpensive.

With any functional needs met by the task lights, the rest of the room can simply be washed with a gentle, low-level illumination furnished by ceiling-mounted downlights, wall-mounted uplights or a pendant lamp. The central position of a pendant lamp means that it will cast shadows, a factor that can make it less appealing than the other alternatives, which, by virtue of multiple globes, produce a dispersed, relatively shadow-free light.

Installing dimmers on room lights maximizes the amount of control you have over the illumination level, turning it up to full when children want to play on their parents' bed in the early evening and dropping it down low when relaxing with a partner at the end of a long day. If possible, have two sets of switches fitted: one at the door and one by the bed. The additional cost is minimal, but the ease of being able to operate the overhead lights without getting out of bed will be a long-term advantage.

❶

❶ Richly colored drapes can be closed across a set of wood-framed glass doors in this bedroom, but the clerestory windows are positioned too high to represent any threat to the room's privacy and therefore require no such screen. Indeed, they play a role in an architectural deception, giving the impression from outside that this house of high-ceilinged rooms actually contains two stories.

❷ Custom-built panels of fixed glazing were installed above a set of wood-framed glass doors, making the most of the room's unusually shaped high ceiling.

❸ A clear acrylic wall allows this room to share space and light with an adjoining corridor. A ceiling-mounted light provides general illumination, but a floor lamp can be used when a gentle glow is preferred.

❷

❸

7

BEDROOM FURNITURE

Whether it is a tailored suite of matching furnishings or an artful
jumble of serendipitous finds, the furniture of the bedroom is
the most tangible expression of its occupants' style. But bedroom
furnishings do more than decorate — they also serve a functional
role, providing storage space for suits, sneakers and sun hats.

BEDROOM FURNITURE

In most bedrooms, the bed is the style cue for the rest of the room. A big brass bed suggests romantic cottage furnishings. A low-lying futon needs Japanese-influenced chests and tables of a similarly sleek line to complement it. An antique bed influences the selection of furniture from a similar period, be it Georgian, Victorian or the popular Arts and Crafts.

Decorating success is relatively easy to achieve when following such a logical strategy. For some of us, though, the whimsical mixing and matching of eclectic style is an irresistible passion, despite the fact that it can be a far harder look to put together. The most reliable course of action is to use pieces that share some common ground in the way of color, shape or pattern. If choosing a diverse selection of wooden furniture, try to work with pieces that have a similar tone: dark woods or blonde woods, but not a hodge-podge of the two. Or if the wood is not really worthy of exhibition, then spruce up the whole collection with a coat of paint in handsome Shaker blue, nostalgic eau de nil or pristine white. You could even match up a rustic, handmade bed sourced from a specialist in Scandinavian antiques with some neat and practical storage pieces from a mass-market manufacturer and finish it all with a pair of modern minimalist reading lamps: the combination can succeed because of the consistently functional aims and pared-back look of the individual items.

PREVIOUS PAGES There are two ways to keep clutter out of the bedroom. One is to stow it all away in custom-built storage drawers and display niches, making storage an inherent part of the structure of the room. The other is to contain it all within a separate room, specially built for storage.

❶ Some people shy away from built-in storage, despite its space-saving qualities, because they are wary of what they perceive to be its mass-produced look. This bedroom shows how just how casual the look can be, facing a purpose-built wardrobe niche with a simple drop of fabric.

❶

❷ In this small bedroom, recessed shelving takes the place of bedside tables, leaving a little more open floorspace around the bed.

❷

STORAGE

A personalized approach to clothes storage usually results in the most space-efficient solutions. If you're having built-in wardrobes made — or if you're trying to make the most of an existing built-in — have a stocktake of your clothes and look at the proportion of shirts, jackets, pants and skirts you need to store in relation to the number of full-length garments, such as coats and dresses. The shorter items usually only require a drop of about 3 feet (1 meter) compared with the roughly 6-foot (2-meter) drop needed for longer items, which means that you can hang double the amount of clothes in the same amount of floorspace, using tiered racks.

The advantage that built-in wardrobes have over freestanding pieces is that they present a uniform facade. Although they may cover as much floorspace as a comparable assortment of freestanding furniture, they don't present the same sort of visual obstruction. As a result, the bedroom feels more spacious and easier to navigate. They can also be designed to make maximum use of the available wall height, climbing all the way to the ceiling if required, a vertical scale that freestanding pieces seldom match.

Some people have a strong aversion to built-in wardrobes and prefer to use freestanding furniture pieces for their bedroom storage. Purpose-built wardrobes are certain to have the right proportions, but if you're interested in co-opting a vintage school locker or an ex-industrial closet, make sure that it has a depth of at least 24 inches (60 cm) to allow room for conventional coat hangers.

Whether you opt for built-in or freestanding clothes storage, focus on making frequently used items as accessible as possible. If you find yourself wasting time by shuffling through a disorganized collection of shoes or T-shirts, then find a way of prioritizing these in your storage scheme. The shoes, for example, might be slipped onto sliding shelves at waist height in the wardrobe, rather than stowed at floor level. The T-shirts, so often lost for months at the back of an overstuffed drawer, might be tucked into pigeonholes, one T-shirt per niche, or even stored on hangers in a separate part of the wardrobe.

Other pieces, including suitcases and trunks, can be used for the storage of infrequently used items, such as heavy winter coats, sweaters or ski clothes. Using the space beneath the bed is a common way of eking out a little extra storage space in the bedroom. Make sure that the stored clothes won't be affected by damp or end up covered in dust: simple cardboard or wicker boxes with lids will do the job in most cases. It's also important to remember that mattresses need good ventilation, so avoid putting too much under the bed.

❶ The paneled door fronts of these built-in wardrobes are in keeping with the room's style and help to camouflage the presence of what is, in fact, a vast amount of storage.

❷ A wooden blade wall forms a galley-style walk-in wardrobe behind the bed, smartly and easily turning a single area into two useful spaces.

❸ It's hard to avoid wasting the space above a wardrobe, but here the gap has been used to best advantage with the display of a collection of basketware.

❹ Built-in storage can be custom made to fit the available space. In this case, closets stretch all the way to the ceiling, maximizing storage capacity.

❸

❹

8

SOFT FURNISHINGS

Drapes, blinds and quilts are the bedroom's finishing touches, the elements that emphasize or enhance the color and character established by furniture pieces and floor and wall coverings. Unlike those larger components, however, soft furnishings also touch the skin, making their selection a tactile as well as a visual choice.

DRAPES AND BLINDS

Drapes and blinds are probably most commonly valued for the contribution they make to the look of the room: think of the different effects created by thick drapes falling from an upholstered box pelmet or a gathered panel of rosy gingham or the smart folds of a Roman blind.

But drapes and blinds are also enormously useful design tools, protecting the privacy of the bedroom's occupants, creating a comfortably dusky environment when daytime rest is necessary, helping to keep a room warm or cool as required and even muffling unwanted sounds.

In most cases, the best way to take advantage of both the functional and decorative qualities of drapes and blinds is to use them in combination. For example, a bedroom located at the front of a single-story row house needs a certain amount of privacy even during daylight hours. A straight drop of a sheer fabric serves as a screen during the day, while still

❷
❸

PREVIOUS PAGES Canopies can be practical things, keeping the environment of the bed snug against wintry drafts or shutting out unwelcome insects in summer. They also, however, have a way of summoning up a romantic mood. Both of these bedrooms make use of those allusions, one with a simple swag of cloth, the other with a more elaborate, but still ornamental, hung canopy.

❶ With their decorative swags and pretty printed drapes, the window dressings help to set the style of the room.

❷ An economic use of fabric sees a box pelmet covered with a distinctive print, while a plain cloth is used for the drapes.

❸ The scale of this wide room suits the deeply opulent swagging of these luxurious window dressings.

allowing the penetration of a reasonable amount of natural light, an advantage in the often dim environment of the row house. On its own, however, the sheer panel is not capable of maintaining privacy after dark when electric lights illuminate the bedroom, nor will it be effective in stopping warmed air from passing out through the window. A set of heavy drapes set in front of the sheer panel will ensure night-time privacy and play an important role in maintaining the temperature of the room.

Simple panel drapes usually hang on an exposed rod. They might be attached to it by rings made from wood, metal or plastic, or by fabric loops or ties. Drapes with a greater amount of decorative detail — pleated and gathered drapes, for example — often run on concealed wall-mounted tracks.

For a more decorative finish, drapes can be mounted within a rigid box pelmet, overhung with a rich swag of fabric or topped with a deep fabric valance. Though they can look rich and luxurious in high-ceilinged rooms, these treatments are best avoided in smaller bedrooms or bedrooms with low ceilings, where they have a tendency to emphasize the shortcomings of the dimensions.

Blinds can either be flat in the manner of a roller blind or a folded Roman blind, or flouncy in the way of a ruched Austrian blind or the even more flamboyant festoon blind.

Drapes and blinds can be made up in a surprising variety of fabrics. A Roman blind, for example, might be made up in raw linen, the fabric's naturally loose weave allowing a welcome dappling of sunlight into the room. Even the basic roller blind has new appeal when made up in a dark-dyed denim or a vintage-style floral.

❶ Roman blinds have an appealing fresh-faced simplicity to them, all the more so when they are made up in a basic cloth, as is the case here. Their inherently trim look is a good match for the neat wooden louvers that also screen these windows.

❷ Tailored bed coverings, such as this fitted quilt, give a finished look to the bedroom, suggesting the high style and superior quality of a glamorous hotel suite.

❸ These window dressings, with their heavy fabric valances, were custom made to suit the character of this period home.

BED FURNISHINGS

The comforter is probably the most popular style of bed cover — and with good reason: it is lightweight but warm, and turns bed-making into the simplest of household chores. Recently, though, there has been a return to vintage fashions in bed-making, a trend that has led to the revival of quilts. The term "quilting" actually refers to the technique of stitching a layer of wadding in between two pieces of fabric, a process that gives the cover better insulating properties. Quilts can be made from plain printed fabrics, but the traditional hand-sewn patchwork quilt is probably the most common.

Bed covers with either fully fitted, pleated or gathered skirts give a trim finish, a look so neat, in fact, that the bed can serve a dual role as a plump bench seat or a day bed. The bed cover is at its most useful in a guest bedroom that doubles as a study or play room, but it can add an air of grand hotel sophistication to any well-furnished bedroom.

Quilts can be either pretty and feminine or grand and formal and are best suited to beds with a nostalgic feel, be they straightforward reproductions or new designs that echo the lines and shapes of old-fashioned beds. The smartly tailored look of a fitted bed cover or the casual dash of color or pattern provided by a good-looking duvet cover teams well with clean-lined contemporary bed designs.

Antique beds are at their best when dressed in a style to suit the period in which they were made. Some period-home decorators long for authenticity, but if you don't want your antique bed to look like it belongs in a museum, the best approach is to use the appropriate covers and canopies, but all in cool, clean white. The all-white scheme will camouflage the extra flounces and give the bed a fresher, more contemporary look.

❷

❸

CHOOSING A MATTRESS

The mattress on which you sleep has an enormous impact on your physical and mental well-being. When a mattress fails to support the weight of your body, your muscles are forced to compensate, leaving you stiff and sore in the morning. Worse still, a restless night of tossing and turning can mean you miss out on the deep sleep that nourishes and rejuvenates.

When shopping for a new mattress, keep in mind that the support provided by the springs and the comfort provided by the padding are two different things. All mattresses should offer good support for the body, but the level of comfort is a matter of personal preference.

The great majority of mattresses have a sprung construction. The old-fashioned hourglass-shaped springs used over a hundred years ago are still the standard in budget-priced mattresses. Better quality mattresses use more complex modes of construction, each with its own advantages to suit different body weights and sleeping arrangements. The basic rule, though, is that the smaller and more numerous the coils, the more effective the mattress will be at supporting you.

The comfort is provided by the padding around the springs. Padding materials are diverse, ranging from simple and inexpensive synthetic fillers to the luxury of latex, a product made from the sap of rubber trees that has natural antibacterial and antifungal properties. As long as you are sure that you are getting good support from your mattress, your choice of comfort level is a matter of taste.

Having bought the best mattress you can afford, you must then take care of it. Even out the wear by turning it over from side to side and end to end every few weeks. At least once a year, take it off the bed and leave it out in the sun to air.

❶ With its layers of patterned fabrics, this room builds up a deep and delicious sense of tactile comfort. Though the treatment is quite lavish, the monochromatic color scheme prevents it being overwhelming.

❶

❷ Different windows often suggest different treatments. Here, smart Roman blinds sit above sash windows, while a generously proportioned drape can be pulled across to cover the French doors when necessary. Coherency is maintained by the use of a single fabric pattern.

❷

9

BEDROOM COLOR

Color is an emotional element, and a highly personal one at that, but it also has specific and indisputable physical properties. Balance the instinctive and the scientific and you will have at your disposal a design tool that can arouse the senses, manipulate spaces and shape your mood.

COLOR

The emotional content of color is perhaps at its most influential in the bedroom, that most intimate of spaces. It is, after all, the room you occupy when you are at your most sensitive, whether at the optimistic dawn of the day or the weary close of night. In such a context, color has the potential to ease the mind, delight the eye or fortify the heart, as you desire.

Most of us have instinctive preferences when it comes to color, yet that intuitive knowledge sometimes abandons us when we are faced with a paint chart. If you find yourself overwhelmed by the sheer number and scope of colors available, you may find it useful to do some homework in order to reconnect with your color instincts. Leaf through some decorating magazines and books and tear out or tag those rooms and color schemes that appeal to you. After a while a pattern should emerge, giving you a clear idea of the colors to which you are drawn and reinforcing your hunches about your personal style. Underlying all that emotional potential is some pure science. Color has some physical characteristics that can't be denied. Indeed, they can be used to your advantage.

Most of us are familiar with the concept that warm colors make large rooms seem smaller and cool colors make small rooms seem larger. This effect can be explained beyond question by science, but in essence it comes down to the relative wavelengths of the colors at either end of the spectrum and how they move through space. The end result is that warm tones literally reach the eye sooner and thus give the impression that they are advancing, drawing surfaces nearer than they really are, and cool tones appear to recede.

It follows, then, that a large bedroom could be made to feel more cozy with a lick of candle-glow gold on the walls.

❶

❶ The blue-and-white color scheme of this bedroom was obviously inspired by its seaside location, but the gray tint to the shade also helps to keep this room feeling cool and fresh, even in the heat and glare of summer.

❷ The palest of gray paint colors used on the feature wall of this bedroom picks up on the steel of the structural columns and on the gnarled bark of the old tree beyond the window. It also gives a note of softness to what is otherwise a very disciplined, very streamlined minimalist interior. ❷

On the other hand, a tiny attic bedroom could be given a coat of crisp, alpine green to give the impression of a lighter, fresher, larger room.

Color can be used to address more specific problems, too. For example, the narrowness of a long thin room can be countered by painting one of the shorter ends in a warm hue, such as an earthy terra cotta or a juicy purple. The warm tone will trick the subconscious into thinking that the surface of the shorter wall is closer than it really is, thus "shortening" the longer walls. Ceiling height can be manipulated in a similar manner, especially if the room has a picture rail running around the walls. Use something like a dark chocolate color above the picture rail and a lighter cocoa below it and the ceiling will seem to sit more snugly. Do the reverse, and an oppressively low ceiling will be given a lift.

It is crucial to remember that color is affected by light. This concept is easiest to understand when you think of the effect daylight has on a stark white wall. In a room filled with sunshine, the pure white surface will take on a yellowish cast. In a room that receives no direct light, that same white surface will have a blue cast. It follows, then, that in a sun-filled room a delicate coral pink could end up looking uncomfortably tropical, and that a sunless room painted in a soft, snowy gray could develop a stark and cold pallor.

The standard decorating advice is to use colors that counteract those conditions, using warm colors in the sunless rooms and cool ones in those that are awash with direct light. The best approach of all is to test your color choices, either by painting a section of the wall (preferably 1 yard/1 meter square or more) or

❶

❶ The innate warmth of this pewter gray is enhanced by the presence of a handsome aubergine in the cushions and the throw rug. The overall result is an essentially neutral color scheme that also manages to be cozy.

❷ Color doesn't only come in a can of paint. Here, soft furnishings are used to introduce a touch of blue.

❸ The owners of this house were keen to maintain its simple, clutter-free aesthetic all the way into their children's bedroom. Though the furnishings and accessories are relatively sparse, the wisteria blue of the walls wraps this pretty little space in charm. With the addition of cushions and blankets in a matching hue, this gentle but rich wall color creates a warm welcome.

❷

❸

① Dark olive tones speak of strength and tradition and are ideally suited to a grand period bedroom. In this instance, a ruby red has been used as an accent color. Red is green's opposite or complementary tone, so the contrast is sure to be striking.

①

② A duck-egg green is the perfect vintage for this lovely old cottage bedroom. Wrapping the color right around all four walls and up across the ceiling magnifies the effect of the hue, making this color look slightly more intense than it would have on the paint chart.

②

by painting a large piece of paper or card that can be propped up somewhere in the room. As the light in the room changes throughout the day, watch how it affects the color sample. Then, at night, take note of how it looks under electric light. After a week or so you should have enough experience with the color to confidently move ahead with your plans — or, of course, to go back to the paint charts and start all over again.

GRAY

The word "gray" is often used to describe something colorless and lifeless, but that is an unkind dismissal of what is in fact a very versatile hue. Gray can have the serenity of a dove, the gravity of the ocean or the lovely depth of burnished pewter.

The grays that appear in a paint chart or in a fabric sample book are often touched by blue or green or purple. Steely blue-grays or military green-grays ought to be seen as cool colors, but rich charcoals or velvety lead colors could exhibit some of the characteristics of a warm color and be used to make a rambling room feel cozier.

Gray tones feature heavily in the ranges of metallic finish paints available. An icy aluminum shade might give an airy, modern, urban look to a bedroom. A lustrous silver could be used to give another space a mood of old-world opulence.

BLUE

Blue is a generous color. It speaks of deep seas and endless skies and all sorts of limitless horizons, from distant mountain tops to faraway forests. It also marries well into many classic color combinations: the cottage charm of blue and yellow, the beachcomber freshness of blue and white or the lovely, liquid depths of blue-green palettes, to name just a few.

More than any other color, blue has the ability to work as either a cool or a warm color. Gray blues, the colors of battleships and snowcaps and urban, industrial landscapes, could be considered cool. Red-tinged blues, the colors often seen in flowers like lavender, cornflowers and delphiniums, have characteristics quite similar to the warm colors. Green blues — tones such as aqua and turquoise — could occupy either camp, depending on their exact make-up, but that injection of yellow tends to give them an eye-catching vibrance, no matter what their precise tone.

This versatility can make working with blues a little trickier than working with reds or purples, but at the same time it means that blue-lovers will be able to find a shade to suit any bedroom, no matter what its proportions or orientation.

GREEN

Like blue, green is a highly adaptable color. When tinged with yellow, as in a lime or a chartreuse, it is lively and vivacious, an animated partner for a lipstick pink or a moody aubergine. When mixed with blue it has the meditative, tranquil quality of a celadon or an eau de nil. When touched by browns or grays to produce various tones of olive, khaki or sage, it can perform like a neutral color: restrained, subtle, sophisticated.

Green is always in favor as a decorating color in studies, living rooms, bathrooms and kitchens, but less so in the bedroom. The reason for this is that some shades of green reflect light in a way that is unflattering for skin tones. Overall, blue greens are kinder than yellow greens, which can be harsh and acidic.

❶

❶ Using different colors in different rooms can be an effective way of personalizing and energizing a home, though there is the risk that the overall result will look a little undisciplined. One way to unify the scheme is to use stark white consistently on ceilings and woodwork throughout the house. The white will highlight the character of the color in each room while providing a sense of flow.

❷ Green has often been used in public buildings, such as libraries, council offices and hospitals. That association has unfairly influenced some people's view of green as a decorating color, but it can be used to good effect, as in this period bedroom.

❸ This very Victorian shade of green imbues a reasonably plain space with a traditional look.

❷

❸

EARTHY ORANGES

Tones of ocher, terra cotta and rust are warm and earthy colors. They might seem uncomfortably fire-licked in an oppressively hot climate, but in most circumstances they feel safe, reassuring, even life-affirming, making them a truly welcome influence in the bedroom.

These orange tones mix well with one another: imagine a room layered in lava and persimmon, for example. Most of the woods used in houses and apartments have similarly rich tones, making those earthy oranges an easy choice in a room with floorboards or parquetry or lots of bare wood detailing around doors and windows.

It can be difficult to find a startling partner for an earthy tone. More often than not, colors such as green, pink and purple look dull beside them. Indeed, it's necessary to look right across to the opposite side of the color wheel to the blues to find a hue capable of matching the innate glow of the earthy oranges. Aqua can be a tantalizing partner to tangerine; navy can look dramatic beside terra cotta. Remember, though, that the clash is a vivid one, capable of disrupting the desired calm of a bedroom. If the drama of contrasting colors appeals, think about minimizing your use of the accent color to a single arm-chair or a pair of pillowcases.

RED

Historically, red has been viewed as a provocative color. It signals passion, danger, rage and celebration. However, color professionals now talk about red as a neutral. They believe that in this increasingly color-aware world, red no longer startles. It regularly works in with the red, white and blue of Italian coastal style and classic Americana. It is a traditional partner of raw linen slub in the south of France. It plays a crisp role in Scandinavian style and a more decadent one in the extravagant

❶ The basic make-up of this vibrant bedroom is rather staid. Walls, carpet and bed linen are rendered in neutral shades. The visual impact comes from the armchair, the rug and the painting. Using these complementary shades as accent colors produces a lively result.

❶

❷ Color can have cultural resonance as well as emotional impact. The Chinese heritage of the owners of this bedroom is expressed in a decor inspired by traditional lacquered jewel boxes. The red niche in which the bed sits provides a vivid and tantalizing contrast to the glossy black that coats the walls, floor and ceiling. ❷

color combinations of the Oriental looks. And it teams up very smartly with any or all of those other classic shades: gray, beige, black and white.

Nonetheless, red still has a stimulating quality that might not be entirely suitable for the bedroom. Stay away from sheer scarlet, and instead look toward yellowish tones, such as coral and lava, or blue tones, such as raspberry. Of course, if you opt for a very blue-affected version of red, for example a dark plum, you may have to stop thinking of it as a warm color and handle it as you would a cool color.

BROWN

After the ubiquitous whites, the brown shades are probably the easiest colors with which to decorate. The lighter versions — beige, taupe, pale clay and so on — are neutrals that provide a little more character than a stark white. They mix well with most shades, from duck-egg blue to mossy green to lavender or dusty red. Yellows and oranges benefit less from the association, as they can look dull in the company of neutral browns.

The darker versions — chocolate, coffee, fudge and nut brown — are high-profile shades, offering the drama and glamour of jet black, with a degree of their own sophistication. They look marvelous in contemporary situations, where they bring just a little warmth to cold elements such as concrete, steel and glass.

Browns work well in layers, which means that they are reliable companions for raw materials such as wood, terra cotta, brick and stone. The great advantage of this is that they can be carried through from a bedroom to a master bathroom with relative ease.

❶

❶ Vast amounts of glazing bring the view and the natural light into the interior of this bedroom. Spaces with these fresh and airy qualities have natural appeal, but they can lack the sense of intimacy that makes a bedroom feel truly inviting. Here, a sizable painting, a patchwork throw and a cushion introduce a palette of cherry, raspberry and marshmallow pink. The blue-tinged reds have a smoky and sensuous look that brings warmth to this cool, modern bedroom.

❷ Soft shades of brown offer something of the depth and coziness of warm colors, such as red and orange, while exhibiting the restraint of a neutral hue.

❸ A dark cocoa feature wall anchors this bed in space and evokes a sense of security.

❷ ❸

BATHROOMS

The modern bathroom has a practical job to do, but it is also
a place in which to relax, a space that can soothe, refresh and
revitalize as well as cleanse. A successful design will address both
function and sensation, thinking logically and laterally in order
to make the most of the room's spatial and sensual potential.

PERFECT BATHROOMS

Not so long ago, the bathroom was little more than a utilitarian component of the house. It was lumped in with other functional but characterless spaces such as the laundry or perhaps the garage, all of them useful but without much in the way of influence. It certainly wasn't seen as the kind of space that might contribute to the mood or the style of the house, let alone enrich the lives of its occupants.

More recently, the bathroom has emerged as a space with an important role to play in the lifestyles of its owners. Open-plan living has changed the modern home, obliterating the dubious distinctions between formal and informal areas, between rooms for living and rooms where the "woman's work" was done. As a consequence, contemporary homes are full of energy and life and activities and conversations that involve all members of the household and their guests. That energy is something to be cherished, but there must be a balance. The bathroom is the space that fulfills an instinctive need for peace and solitude. No longer just a place to wash hair and brush teeth, the bathroom now offers a retreat from the public domain, a private sanctuary much needed in a world full of visual, aural, professional and social stimuli.

Of course, just as those open-plan living spaces need to function well in order to fulfill their potential, so too must the bathroom perform its duties efficiently and effectively before its role as a domestic sanctuary can be realized.

PREVIOUS PAGES The modern bathroom is a personal pleasure dome, but that concept is very much open to interpretation. For some it may mean being surrounded by opulent colors and finishes. For others it could mean the modest indulgence of watching television in the bath.

❶ Bathtubs come in all shapes and sizes but, whatever model you choose, you will need to factor in some additional floorspace for getting into and out of the tub. A strip of space at least 28 inches (700 mm) deep is the bare minimum.

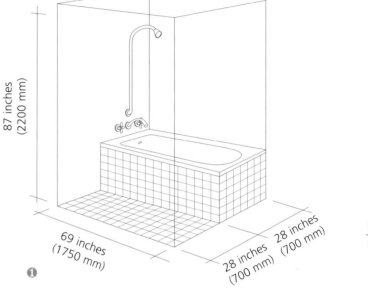

❷ An uncluttered floorplan and a stark black-and-white palette combine in a bathroom blissfully free of decorative stimuli.

❸ Quirky fittings and fixtures give this bathroom a sense of edgy whimsy.

❹ A purely decorative fabric canopy brings a dash of style to a rustic bathroom.

❺ A table converted into a vanity unit represents a softer, more furnished approach to bathroom decorating, evidence that the utility of the space is no longer the priority.

No one can relax, let alone feel pampered or nurtured, in a bathroom where the faucets drip, the water temperature goes up and down, the lights glare, the shower floods, the towels never dry and you have to step over the toilet to reach the tub.

In recent years, designers have started approaching the design of the bathroom in terms of zones. By definition, the number and nature of these zones will depend on the size and shape of the individual bathroom and the requirements of those using it. They might, however, include a grooming zone around the vanity, a showering zone that could take the form of an independent shower room and a bathing zone that might also include an open fire or access to a courtyard. Space can limit some of these possibilities, but even the smallest of bathrooms can be artfully sectioned to make best use of the available area. Freestanding walls housing electrical wiring and plumbing that can be used to screen one part of the bathroom from the other are an extraordinarily effective and popular way of altering floorplans in the modern bathroom.

Once the structure has been decided, it's time to indulge in the visual and tactile pleasures of shopping for surface materials, fittings and accessories. This is where the bathroom has the potential to transcend its functional role, to become a place that actively soothes and restores those who use it. Color, of course, is a key element, capable of setting a mood and even influencing emotions. Texture, too, plays a part. So does lighting. Practical considerations affect these choices, too, as some materials are simply not hardy enough for the moist atmosphere of the bathroom and electricity must be handled with due deference to the risks inherent in a wet room. But even within these parameters the possibilities are vast. One person might yearn for the ethereal depths of luminous glass tiles, another for the folksy feel of dappled light falling on polished wood, another for a grotto of jade-green mosaics.

❶ When drawing up the bathroom floor-plan, make sure there is at least a clearance of 28 inches (700 mm) in front of the shower. This is the space you will use before showering when you stand outside and test the water temperature, and after showering when you step outside to towel dry.

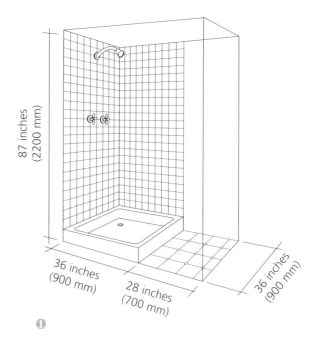

❶

❷ Copper-clad walls and glass mosaic tiles completely outshine the modest nature of this over-the-bath shower. Materials such as these are not inexpensive, but they do illustrate that space need not inhibit a rich sense of style.

❷

❶ A solid blade wall clad in marble and topped with a glass panel divides this handsome bathroom into two zones. To the rear is a double shower, accessible from either end. To the fore is a spacious bathing and grooming area, which takes full advantage of a dramatic view.

❷ Vanities can be very petite indeed but even the smallest of hand basins requires a reasonable amount of elbow room.

❸ This warm-climate bathroom also breaks down the space into functional zones, and an additional shower zone is actually located outside the room in a walled courtyard.

❹ A small counter tailor-made for the application of make-up was installed in this bathroom. A conventional vanity with a hand basin stands on the opposite wall.

❸

❹

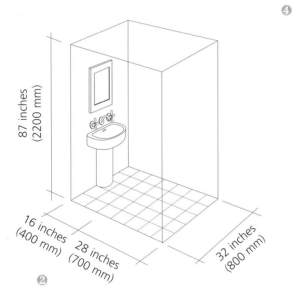

87 inches (2200 mm)

16 inches (400 mm) 28 inches (700 mm) 32 inches (800 mm)

❷

❶

MODERN BATHROOMS

Modern bathrooms are defined not so much by a particular look,
as by a set of ideas: that a bathroom should be a place of sanctuary,
that it should be aesthetically and functionally in tune with the
lifestyles of its owners, and that it should reflect a respect for,
and a sense of connection with, the natural environment.

MODERN BATHROOMS

In the last few decades our lifestyles have led to changes in the way we build and use our homes, including the way we design our bathrooms.

In a busy and sometimes impersonal world, the home has become a place of refuge. Within the home, the bathroom is seen as a retreat, a place in which to restore both mind and body. This approach is applied to most modern bathrooms, and yet the manner in which the idea manifests itself can vary enormously from one example to the next.

The bathing rituals of the Romans, the Turks, the Scandinavians and the Japanese are the inspiration for many modern Western bathrooms. Some feature sunken tubs and steam rooms inside bathrooms of vast proportions. Others dot the ceiling with fiber-optic lights that evoke the pleasures of bathing under a starlit sky. Others are more high-energy, incorporating the invigorating pleasures of body-pounding showers and baths with powerful directional water jets.

PREVIOUS PAGES This modern, meditative space is typical of contemporary bathrooms in that it has strong connections with the natural environment. In structural terms, it extends beyond the four walls of the house to include a courtyard area with a spa pool, but it also emphasizes its links with the landscape by using building materials that occur naturally in the area.

❶

❶ Influenced by the dimensions of traditional Japanese soaking tubs, the limestone-clad bath is a full 3 feet (1 meter) deep.

❷ Taken individually, the materials used here could almost be described as rustic: wood, limestone and sandblasted concrete blocks. Here, they combine with sleek shapes to produce a mellow and organic interpretation of clean-lined minimalism. Note, too, that the wall behind the vanity has been finished in plaster. Its stony tint was mixed in by hand to yield an uneven distribution of color, a mottled effect that allows the surface to blend with the other natural materials used in the bathroom.

❸ A shower fitting is fixed to a solid wall clad in limestone, with a second, oversized showerhead extending from the ceiling.

❷

❸

Many contemporary bathrooms look outward, taking in the views and the natural light that were shunned by the highly protective, inward-looking bathrooms of old. Some even physically reach out into exterior areas, incorporating wide openings such as French doors or fully retractable walls, so that, while in the tub, bathers can feel the soft breezes and perhaps even the gentle sunlight of the world outside. Others in warm climates include external showers, usually tucked inside a courtyard or a garden protected by walls or hedges, but otherwise exposed to the fresh air and glowing sun.

The windows above this tub allow the bather to gaze out over harbor waters. Extensive use of glazing on the walls and on the vanity cabinet brings the harborside atmosphere into the bathroom itself. Tumbled marble tiles were used on the floor and the bath surround, their earthy, clay tones working to ground the ethereal look of the room.

Contemporary bathrooms also tend to challenge the conventional bathroom floorplan, which calls for all the major fixtures to be arranged against the walls of the room. Blade walls are commonly used to define spaces according to function and to restore some of the privacy lost to generous windows and floor-to-ceiling glazing. For example, a free-standing wall might be stationed in the center of the room, separating the vanity area from the bathing area. The vanity, installed on the wall facing the door, can then be used by one person without disturbing the solitude of another in the shower or bathtub behind the blade wall.

One thing that all contemporary bathrooms should embrace is environmentally sound technology. Water-saving shower-heads, toilets and faucets are easy to source, and well-designed floorplans that make the most of natural light and ventilation can reduce energy consumption.

❶

❷

❶ A few clever deceptions were required to give this relatively small master bathroom a feeling of roominess. Mirrors obviously create the illusion of extra space, but a more interesting strategy was the designer's decision to clad the walls and floor in a dark limestone that focuses attention onto the stark white marble of the vanity area. This manipulation allows the surrounding walls to recede from view.

❷ The sculptural quality of this vanity clearly makes it the centerpiece of the room. The distinctive basins are made from black glass.

❸ A freestanding wall separates the bathing area from the toilet.

❸

❶

❶ Colorful ceramic tiles make a splendid contrast with the very somber black, white and gray of the rest of the bathroom. The open shower has been designed so that water flows down the oversized steps and into the sunken bath.

❷ This dynamic, unmistakably modern bathroom was inspired by the bathing traditions of the ancient Romans. The very deep, sunken tub is reached by a series of steps, a structure reminiscent of the Roman baths still in existence in Britain. A skylight above matches the dimensions of the bath and allows a direct view of the sky, a set-up intended to recreate the ambiance of outdoor bathing. Concrete, a material invented by the Romans, was used on the floor and vanity counter to recreate the feeling of an ancient Roman bath.

❷

❶

❶ A custom-made concrete bath surround matches the loose curves of this bathroom. The concrete was tinted to match the tone of the glass mosaic tiles used on the floor and walls. The stainless steel toilet was sourced, unusually, from a penitentiary supply store.

❷ Installed in the open living spaces of a quirky and unconventional city loft, this bathroom was designed as a freestanding, amorphously shaped, independent cell. The solid walls stop just short of the ceiling and the gap is filled with glazing. As a result, the space retains a visual connection with the apartment and makes the most of the natural light entering through the external windows.

❷

❶ In a manner typical of contemporary bathrooms, this space uses a freestanding wall to divide the room into zones. The space on one side of the wall is utilitarian, containing the vanity area, the toilet and the shower recess. The other side is occupied solely by an elegantly stepped bathtub.

❷ The key to this bathroom's success is the construction of the defining blade wall. The solid part of the wall houses all the plumbing, with faucets on either side variously serving the hand basins, the shower and the tub. The horizontal section is clad in small white tiles, while the vertical stretch is clad in larger, dewy melon-green tiles. The contrast contributes to a sense of spaciousness by distinctly emphasizing the room's breadth and height.

❸ Two pairs of interlocking wooden strips serve as a screen, completing the sense of separation between the two zones while maintaining a visual connection. The rich color of the wood balances the cool tones of the tiles used on the bathroom's vertical and horizontal surfaces.

❷

❸

❶

❶

❶ A dramatic cliff-face location presented some challenges for the designer of this house. The family bathroom, for example, had to be located on the side of the house that butts up to the cliff. As a result, the room has no external windows. To allow light into the space, the designer used an almost fully glazed ceiling. A mirror installed on the blade wall facing the door reflects the ocean view visible through the windows of a nearby living area.

❷ Gray grouting was used throughout the bathroom to accentuate the graphic nature of the broad white floor and wall tiles and the smaller blue glass mosaic tiles of the blade wall.

❷

❶

❶ Refurbishing spaces designed by esteemed architects is always a delicate and contentious business. Here, the challenge was to remodel bathrooms in a building designed by Ludwig Mies van der Rohe in the 1940s. The brilliant and innovative solution was to install a free-standing, boat-shaped room that does not disturb the basic structure of the original building. The external glass wall of the master bathroom faces the bedroom. On the reverse side, a guest bathroom concealed behind a wall of teak panels serves the living areas.

❷ The materials used for the room — namely glass, steel, stone and teak — are typical of Mies van der Rohe's own work.

❷

The overwhelming shift toward aesthetic self-expression and individual taste — another of those late 20th-century cultural changes — makes any discussion of the style of contemporary bathrooms close to meaningless. By definition, modern bathrooms are tailor-made to suit the tastes and tendencies of their owners: they might gleam with lustrous glass mosaic tiles, glint with stainless steel or smolder with the warm tones of organic materials such as wood or terra cotta. Some will exhibit the sleek, spare lines of minimalism; others will take a rococo mirror from here, a 1960s plastic storage unit from there, a complete suite of cutting-edge bathroom hardware from a specialist design shop, tie it up with fairy lights and celebrate the well-informed eclecticism of it all.

❶ The liberating decision to forgo a tub altogether in this small bathroom made it possible to include an expansive double shower in the rear section of the space.

❷ Vanities installed on blade walls are usually visible through an open door. To honor that prominence, they are often designed as showpieces, with sculptural qualities that go beyond their functional purpose.

❸ The blade wall forms the fourth wall of the shower area, with entrances at either end. All vertical surfaces are clad in the same sea-green mosaic tiles, a uniform treatment that gives this space an underwater quality.

❷

❸

❶

❶

❷

❸

❶ The tones of the floor tiles, the marble used for the bath surround and the paint color used on the walls are consistent with the hues of the nearby master bedroom.

❷ In the contemporary bathroom, the showering experience can be every bit as luxurious as that afforded by a relaxing bath. In this case, the shower recess has been designed as a sumptuous steam room.

❸ Mirror-fronted cabinets blur the boundaries of the room, helping to create an impression of spaciousness. The reflective surfaces also make the most of the natural light entering through a skylight above the bathtub.

❹ Tiles laid on the diagonal have a broadening effect in the long, narrow bathroom. Similarly, the curves of the bath surround, the vanity counter and the dressing table soften the inherent angularity of the space.

❹

❶ This is another example of how a blade wall has been used to section a bathroom into different zones. In this case, the wall has created a public zone, visible from the broad opening made by the Japanese-style doors, and a private zone to the rear, which includes a shower and a toilet.

❶

❷ Separate rooms for the shower and the toilet are anchored to the free-standing wall. This very functional area has its own pedestal basin. The more picturesque vanity installed on the reverse side of this blade wall has a largely decorative purpose.

❷

❶

❷

❶ Stainless steel is often used in modern
bathrooms. It is waterproof and resistant
to heat, making it a sound choice in the hot,
moist environment of the bathroom. However,
it is not an inexpensive material by any means.
One solution is to combine stainless steel with
look-alike materials, such as laminate. Here,
a gray laminate has been used on the vanity
as a partner to the stainless steel basin. It is
also possible to source laminates that have
a reflective, metallic finish.

❷ This polished chrome tower provides just
as much storage space as a more conventional
piece of cabinetry but without the visual bulk,
an important consideration in this compact
space. Chrome insets dot the white wall tiles,
picking up on the stylish gleam of the tower.
The parallel lines of chrome insets that
encircle the room at dado height are matched
by a single line close to the ceiling, a device
that draws the eye up and again enhances
the sense of space.

③

④

③ The aim in this bathroom was to bring a healthful, outdoor look into an enclosed room. A skylight installed above the shower floods the space with natural light. Glass mosaic tiles were selected for the walls because of their ability to reflect sunlight, causing glints and sparkles that bring movement and vitality to the space. The concrete of the floor and vanity counter contributes an earthiness, but also makes reference to the bathroom's urban context.

④ To make this small bathroom appear as spacious as possible, a decision was made not to install shower screens. For this to work, it was necessary to ensure that nearby fittings and finishes were waterproof; note that the wooden cabinetry is shielded from the shower by a short blade wall. A raised section of the floor confines the shower water.

NOSTALGIC BATHROOMS

Bathrooms in spaces of a distinct architectural style can remain true to the spirit of their surrounds without necessarily taking on the heavy burden of authenticity. Be as accurate as possible with color and character, but be confident about taking advantage of modern design ideas to create a room that feels as good as it looks.

PREVIOUS PAGES A nostalgia for times past can be honored in all sorts of spaces, whether they are original period bathrooms, rooms once used for other purposes inside an old house or apartment, or new rooms built from scratch. The traditional character can be conveyed by large architectural features, such as lead glass windows, or by smaller details, such as antique furnishings.

❶ A complete renewal of an old bathroom was achieved without any loss of character by replacing heavy polished wooden cabinetry, dark wallpaper and dark carpet with daintily detailed painted cabinetry, a moss-green Venetian stucco wall finish and a fine floor of natural stone. The addition of two skylights also brings a much-needed dose of daylight into the room. A clever floorplan, which uses freestanding vanities and a blade wall to separate the storage area from the body of the bathroom, gives this sprawling space the more intimate ambiance of a number of small, furnished rooms.

❷ Little details, including the faucets and light fittings, give an air of authenticity to the newly furnished room.

❸ An abundance of custom-built storage in the bathroom is definitely a contemporary notion, but the shape of the mirrored door panels and the large number of tiny drawers give this cabinetry an elegant, traditional look.

❷

❸

❶

For true enthusiasts, old homes — be they Victorian cottages, Art Deco apartments, neo-Gothic mansions or something far humbler — are more than a place to live, they're a lifestyle. The bricks and mortar and turned wooden railings embody not just an architectural style, but an atmosphere that their modern-day owners would like to see represented in every room of the house.

This is, of course, a comparatively easy task in a dining room or a bedroom, where household rituals have changed little over the course of the years. A bathroom, however, presents special challenges. All but the most slavish of period devotees would agree that functional modern developments must be incorporated: things such as hot and cold running water, electric lights, heating, ventilation, freestanding showers and indoor toilet suites. Most would also be persuaded to make room for social trends that see us treating the bathroom as a space in which

❶ This bathroom tackles the problem of combining the new and the old head on. To turn this old bedroom into a bathroom, a wall of joinery was installed at right angles to the exterior wall, leaving the generous volume of the room untouched. On one side of it is the vanity, on the other the tub.

❷ The vanity's lean and lightweight design, including open niches and a cantilevered counter, exposes the grand dimensions and intricate detailing of the original room.

❸ Cabinets stand at right angles to the vanity wall, forming a neat corridor between the two zones and limiting the obstruction to period details, such as baseboards and windowsills.

❶

❶ The traditional styling of the wooden cabinetry belies its contemporary approach to storage capacity and accessibility.

❷ The painted mural on the ceiling is a sentimental element. It was designed to bring something of the surrounding woodlands into the bathroom itself, but it also pays homage to an era when such decorative fancies were more commonplace.

to spend lovely, leisurely personal time, a change that may influence the installation of a spa bath, a double shower or a comfortable walk-in closet.

Bathrooms in period houses often have architectural features that bestow on the room a rather wonderful sense of place. Existing bathrooms may have a splendid claw-foot bathtub or some elegant vanity cabinetry that can become the center-piece for the refurbished room.

Remember, too, that there is nothing to stop the modern owner of a period house from rearranging the floorplan and using an old bedroom or drawing room as the venue for a new, though nostalgically styled, bathroom. These spaces can include fireplaces, chandeliers, balconies, wooden shutters — all sorts of fixtures and trims that contribute to an evocative bathroom, but are also deliciously idiosyncratic.

❷

❸ This new bathroom was specifically designed to have some of the qualities of the 20th-century Arts and Crafts style. The key to the look is the bay window, its presence enhanced by a barrel-vault ceiling. Windows feature traditional brass lights and the raised panels of the maple cabinetry around the tub recall the fine woodwork of the era.   ❸

Many manufacturers of bathroom hardware have ranges that cater specifically for traditional bathrooms, reproducing the original styles of faucets, spouts, bathtubs, hand basins and light fittings in high-quality contemporary materials.

Utilizing these modern remakes is certainly the easiest course of action, but it is also possible to track down authentic pieces from specialist dealers or from salvage yards. These may need resurfacing, a treatment that can add considerably to the base price of the item. They may also be more difficult for modern plumbers, electricians and builders to handle, so they could add to the cost of building work.

Paint manufacturers, too, produce ranges that tie in with a variety of architectural styles, making it easy to find a historically suitable hue for a period bathroom.

The decoration of this bathroom was inspired by an elegant English antique located elsewhere in the master suite. The intention was to give this space a furnished look. The most influential element is without doubt the custom-made cabinetry, with its double-arch cathedral doors and decorative paneling.

②

③

④

❶ In contrast to most contemporary vanities, the cabinetry features many small drawers. It's a style tactic employed to relate the new piece to the impeccably detailed antiques on show in this master suite. The glass doors permit the display of a collection of antique perfume bottles.

❷ The very best bathroom designs are those that connect with the needs of their owners. In this case, the faucet was set unusually high to accommodate the owner's preference for washing her hair in a basin.

❸ Powder-blue wallpaper with a decorative chinoiserie pattern is a soft, feminine and rather whimsical choice in a room of nostalgic charm.

❹ A heavy drape has been used to allow the privacy that might otherwise be provided by a door or a screening wall.

❶

❶ A set of antique table lamps was modified and installed as a pair of stylish wall sconces framing the dressing table.

❷ Without adhering to any particular stylistic period, the dark-stained wooden cabinetry nonetheless expresses a strong sense of tradition. Fabric panels behind nickel-plated wire mesh contribute to that mood.

❸ Located in its own vestibule, the luxuriously proportioned tub is undoubtedly the focal point of the bathroom.

❶

❷

❸

❹ This bathroom was designed to have a very formal, very traditional air, without reference to any specific period or style. Vintage furniture pieces from Africa and Asia and a few European antiques are layered with sumptuous new fittings to build up a look of well-traveled eclecticism.

❹

❶ Bathrooms of past eras were usually utilitarian spaces, despite the sometimes magnificent qualities of their architectural style. One way of bringing a contemporary attitude into a bathroom with a traditional look is to take inspiration from other period spaces, such as drawing rooms and bedrooms. Here, an armchair, a framed mirror and an elaborate light fitting invite the bather to use this bathroom as a living space, too.

❷ Patterned wallpaper and some architectural detail make a suitable but subtle backdrop for this splendidly restored claw-foot bathtub. The addition of elements such as the drapes, the framed print and the fine reproduction chair bring a livable quality to this functional room.

❸

❹

❸ Some clever design deceptions and an assortment of luxurious fittings and materials make a little palace out of this petite apartment bathroom. Though it doesn't strictly belong to any traditional style of bathroom, the gilt-framed mirror is responsible for much of the room's character. It is partnered with a reproduction bath and faucets. The convex mirror subverts the sense of space, distracting the eye from the room's small dimensions.

❹ Aside, perhaps, from the shaded light fittings, there is nothing in this bathroom that could be described as "authentically period." The custom-made vanity cabinets, the frameless mirror, the tumbled marble tiles and the spa bath are all contemporary features, yet a graceful air of vintage elegance flourishes. The paneling of the vanity doors is a persuasive element. So, too, is the ornate style of the brass faucetry.

❶ Handpainted wreaths of gold around the basin, on the door fronts and on the outside of the bath enhance the sparkling detail of the glass wall sconces and the gleaming metallic wall finish. They also show a commitment to decorative embellishment rarely seen in contemporary bathrooms.

❶

❷ The style of this splendidly esoteric bathroom has been described by its owners and creators as "country-house glam." Elements such as the claw-foot bath and the Georgian corner cabinet, its somber tones matched by the stained wooden floorboards, are very literally traditional. So, too, is the tub's faucetry, a reproduction French hand-held shower fitting not installed on the wall but plumbed through the floor as it would have been in the days when interior rooms were first converted into working bathrooms. Other elements are simply evocative, such as the metallic paint finish overlaid with a lattice of patterned wallpaper strips. The treatment has the glow of old pewter and the detail of fine filigree.

❷

13

CLASSIC BATHROOMS

By definition, classic bathrooms are fashion-neutral, but that doesn't mean they have to be personality-free. They may have the aristocratic air of cool marble, the burnished good looks of wood or the rustic chic of hand-cut, matte-glazed tiles. Whatever their style, the one thing they must embody is a sense of ageless beauty.

PREVIOUS PAGES The aesthetic neutrality of the classic bathroom doesn't cancel out its luxurious potential. Materials with remarkable textures and grains bring their distinctive qualities to the classically styled space without compromising its simplicity.

❶ Shower walls of frameless glass keep the focus on the bathroom's handsome structure and striking graphic detailing.

❷ The high contrasts of a black-and-white color scheme bring visual dynamism to a space — not a quality normally associated with classic bathrooms. Yet this is a classic color combination, one that endures regardless of fashion. It also reflects the urban perspective of this city apartment.

❸ The contrasting black tiles are inlaid with fragments of mother-of-pearl. This tiny detail is the exquisite touch that brings intimacy and sophistication to an otherwise rather masculine bathroom.

❹ A private room, separated from the main body of the bathroom by a pocket door, contains the toilet.

CLASSIC BATHROOMS

The classic bathroom is a surprisingly cunning space. Its aesthetic neutrality gives it the power to bridge stylistic gaps, a quality that many renovators find highly desirable. The need to resolve the disparate identities of an original structure and new building work is always a challenge, whether the project involves the wholesale gutting of a 19th-century cottage, the updating of a 1920s Italianate apartment or the extension of a 1960s family home. Without being burdened by the gravity of authenticity, the classically styled bathroom can still embody a timelessness that assures its compatability with the original building. And at the same time it can have the fresh, light qualities that we associate with contemporary architecture.

❶ Storage issues must be handled carefully in a classic bathroom. If there is too little storage space, there will probably be a spill of clutter onto vanity counters and windowsills. But if the storage unit is too large, it can be visually overwhelming. Here, the capacity of a well-proportioned vanity is supplemented by more storage space concealed behind the mirrors.

❷ The simple styling of the faucets should withstand the vagaries of fashion.

❸ The eye rests easy when contrasts between colors and materials are minimal. In this case, the same Italian limestone has been used on the floors, on the walls above and below the cantilevered vanity, and as a vanity counter.

❶ The aim of classic bathroom design is to produce a space that will look as good in five or ten years' time as it does the day it is built. In this case, the bathroom has been clad in black, an unorthodox choice, but nonetheless a color that could be described as classic.

❷ Marble has a marvelous capacity to read either as a traditional material or a modern one. It is associated with bathing rituals as far back as the ancient Greeks and Romans. Its decorative veining can be used effectively in ornate period interiors, and yet its cool, clean-cut look suits the pared-back nature of many modern bathrooms. It is this versatility that makes it an excellent choice in a classic bathroom. Here, it provides a link between the structure of a modern bathroom and the gracious home in which it is installed.

❸ The floor tiles have been laid on the diagonal, a tactic that unites the gentle curve of the window with the more austere lines of the newly built vanity and shower. Note, too, how the rounded bath surround balances the shape of the bay window and softens the blunt lines of the nearby cabinetry.

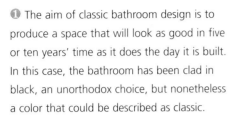

❷

❸

❶

❶

A classic bathroom is also a pragmatic choice if you want to protect the resale value of your property, an issue that applies to entirely new houses and apartments as well as refurbishments. A well-executed classic bathroom is likely to appeal to the majority of prospective buyers, whether the property is to be sold now or in ten years' time.

To be truly classic rather than low-key, a bathroom must be entirely fad-free. Following trends in color, materials, hardware or light fittings will date the bathroom and undermine the space's sense of calm, composed, ageless style.

❶ Installed in a narrow terrace in a historic neighborhood, this elegant space manages to reflect its environment while still providing its owners with a light and relatively spacious master bathroom. Details such as the shaded lights, the paneled cabinetry and the moldings around the doors impart a graceful sense of age, while the cream tones used throughout the room prevent the traditional elements becoming too dominant.

❷ A classic bathroom demands subtlety, especially when it comes to storage issues. Here, additional storage space is built into the walls that bracket the vanity area, but their featureless door fronts suggest nothing more than decorative paneling.

❷

❸ All-white color schemes are easy to execute and can be relied upon to produce a smart, fresh look. However, as this bathroom shows, an accent color gives a little more character to the space without inhibiting the room's classic style.

❹ Integrated elements, such as the storage nooks seen reflected in the vanity mirror, are a good choice in a classic bathroom. They eliminate the need for additional fittings and fixtures that may date the bathroom.

❸   ❹

❶

❶ In this instance, the all-white color scheme has been given a dose of character and a lick of warmth by the use of wood, not only in the upright storage unit, but in the frames of the window and skylights.

❷ This bathroom benefits from contemporary ideas about the need for ample quantities of natural light, hence the skylights set into the ceiling. The simplicity of the elements — from the frameless glass shower surround to the handsome hand basins — give this bathroom a timeless quality that will last.

❷

❶ A combination of open nooks, cabinet space and sliding drawers provides storage areas for the medicines and toiletries that need to be concealed, as well as display areas for the beautiful accessories that the bathroom often collects.

Achieving a fashion-neutral bathroom certainly requires a clear head. Start by looking at the materials that have been used in bathrooms quite literally for centuries: marble, wood and tiles. Relative newcomers such as steel and terrazzo are probably best avoided. Even some of the stones have style affiliations that make them problematic in a classic bathroom, despite their credentials as materials of high quality and long endurance. Granite, for example, will always be associated with the 1980s, while limestone, a gracefully handsome material to be sure, might yet become stylistic shorthand for late 20th-century minimalism.

❷

❷ This heated ladder towel rack warms the towels, of course, but it is also used to take the chill off the bathroom in winter.

❸ Color can be used in the classic bathroom, but it must be handled with care. Combinations of colors — aside from the timeless classics, such as black and white or blue and white — are prone to date easily. A more prudent strategy is to use a single color throughout. Here, the same blue tiles have been used on the floor, the walls and the bath surround. ❸

❶ This subtle space demonstrates how the classic bathroom's neutrality can translate into aesthetic flexibility. Here, sheer Austrian blinds with a deep printed valance are a feminine touch that gives the bathroom a well-dressed finish. With the window dressings dismantled, the space regains its elegant simplicity.

❷ Purpose-built wet rooms that eliminate the need for intrusive shower screens are a recognizable design feature of contemporary bathrooms. In the classic bathroom, floor-to-ceiling panels of glass make for a comparably low-profile shower area.

❸ Flat-faced cabinetry might look fresh in the bathroom of a contemporary house or apartment, but it can be out of place in an older home. Paneled door and drawer fronts, such as the ones used in this bathroom, can convey a sense of age without committing to any specific architectural period.

❶

❷

❸

It can be hard to detect the traces of contemporary fashion in bathtubs, basins, toilet suites, lights and faucetry. The soundest course of action is to opt for simplicity, avoiding extremes — the brutally square-cut fittings designed for sharp-edged modern bathrooms and the curls and loops of organically styled fittings meant for more fanciful spaces.

Color need not be an outcast in a classically styled space, though shades of white and cream will always be the most reliable choices. Tones inspired by nature at its most gentle — stony gray, soft sand and the blue-green of seaside rock-pools — offer a sense of constancy that ought to see out the life of the bathroom.

❶

❷

❶ This bathroom is unmistakably influenced by traditional styling: it's evident in the turned legs, the bead-board paneling, the hexagonal floor tiles and, of course, the claw-foot bath. Despite that, it avoids the visual heaviness of some traditional bathrooms thanks to a fresh and elegant cream-on-white color scheme.

❷ The broad bench seat in the shower, the frameless glass screen and the storage niches framed by decorative tiles are evidence of how contemporary thinking in a traditional context can produce a modern classic.

❸ The gilded mirror is a confident touch that gives a little pizzazz to this very refined space.

❸

❶ This bathroom was installed in a new house designed along the lines of the Spanish Colonial homes of 19th-century California. This very specific style reference is evident in the mosaic border tile and in the oil-rubbed bronze faucetry. The muted palette of the room and the inclusion of sleek contemporary features such as the frameless glass shower and the custom-made banquette swing the balance back toward the contemporary, ultimately achieving an aesthetic neutrality.

❷ This angled vanity is an excellent solution in a small bathroom. The tapering line ensures that there is room to move at the entrance to the shower, while the open construction maintains sightlines through to the wall, making the most of the available volume in a visual sense. Because it is so pragmatic and because it has been created in quality materials in a neutral palette, this vanity will always look well suited to its bathroom and will therefore never look dated.

③

④

③ A frameless mirror, a vanity of strikingly simple construction and a clean, clear glass panel serving as a screen for the over-the-bath shower are all neutral elements in this classically styled space.

④ For a classic bathroom, this space shows an unusual amount of personality. The bathtub and vanity have cool, clear, unobtrusively modern lines, yet they are clearly influenced by the vintage of the old beach house in which this bathroom sits. The look is loosely sentimental, but not at all old-fashioned.

① ②

④

① A wall of glass bricks allows natural light to penetrate into the shower area during the day. At night it reflects the artificial light, forming a warm, glowing backdrop to the bathroom's luxurious tub.

② It was necessary to lighten the visual bulk of the bathroom's twin vanity to prevent it becoming an imposing mass. The solution was to set the granite counter above the maple-fronted cabinetry, using small stainless steel rods as supports.

③ Shelves and a bench seat are integrated elements of the shower. They make use of an awkwardly shaped area without disturbing the shower's low-key, monochromatic design.

④ The color palette, rendered in granite, wood and stone, is limited to soft shades of malt and caramel. These colors give warmth to the room's simple, classic shapes and lines.

❶ A gently curving bay window is a dramatic backdrop for this spacious bath. Frosted glass panels provide privacy, but still permit obscured views of the garden outside the window. That hazy visual is echoed by the beautiful nude painted on glass that sits on the bath surround.

❷ The vintage French light fittings used around the vanities and the bathtub give the room an elegant sense of age without limiting it to any specific decorative era.

❶

❷

❸ This is another example of how a bathroom of subtle coloring and simple styling can nonetheless be an interesting, distinctive room. In this case, the element of difference is provided by a three-dimensional geometric pattern displayed on the lower panels of the vanity and in the white tiles scattered across the wall. The whimsical way in which the feature tiles are deployed from dado to ceiling is one of the bathroom's most appealing features.

❸

14

CHARACTER BATHROOMS

One room in the house that affords the opportunity for a bit
of decorating fun is the bathroom. It's a space used for little
more than an hour at a time, a space where you can indulge
a stylistic whim without fear of regret. This is your chance to
visit the Valley of the Kings or dive to the bottom of the ocean.

AN EGYPTIAN FANTASY

This theatrical bathroom is the most extreme manifestation of the character bathroom, capable of carrying you away not only to another place but to another time. The murals on the walls are historically accurate, and reproduced in the style of the early Egyptian dynasties. The columns are inscribed with hieroglyphs, including renderings of the owners' names. And the owners' collection of Egyptian curios is displayed in museum-style cabinets throughout the bathroom and the attached bedroom. An Art Deco influence gives an undercurrent of glamour to the heavily themed space, recalling the opulent interiors of Hollywood in its Golden Years or Las Vegas in its decadent infancy. It's extravagant, it's indulgent, but it's undeniably a luxurious world unto itself.

PREVIOUS PAGES Character bathrooms exist independently of design evolution and, as a result, they never really go out of style. From the gilded chandelier to the showcase circular tub, this bathroom is an expression of decadence that will never date.

❶ The circular tub is the centerpiece of the bathroom. It is ringed by a tiered marble surround detailed with geometric inlays.

❷ Reproductions of ancient Egyptian murals encircle the room above dado height.

❸ The patterning on the vanity mirror is evidence of the room's Art Deco influences and picks up on the look of decorative sandblasted glass panels used as privacy screens elsewhere in the bathroom.

❶

❶ Jet-black columns frame the entrance to the bathroom from the bedroom. The sandblasted glass screen with papyrus-reed detailing ensures that there are no direct views into the bathing area.

❷ Soaring decorative columns enhance the extraordinary scale of this massive bathroom. The fiberglass shells were filled with concrete on site, then painted with bands of hieroglyphs. The owners' extensive collection of Egyptian curios is housed in glass-fronted cabinets lodged between columns on the perimeter of the bathroom.

❷

1 Enhancing the delightful tree-house aspect of this mellow space is a beaded Moroccan panel, sandwiched between two pieces of glass and used as a shower screen.

1

GARDEN BATHROOMS

One of the most significant developments in contemporary home design has been the blurring of the boundaries between interior and exterior spaces. Nowhere has this had more sensual results than in the bathroom.

Only a couple of decades ago, the idea of including a view-catching window in a bathroom would have been considered a little risqué — after all, the bathroom was seen as a private and essentially functional space, not a space in which to sit back and enjoy a pleasant outlook.

These days, it's not unusual to see a pair of folding windows set beside a deep bath offering voluptuous views of a land-scaped garden. Indeed, a panel of glazing in the exterior wall of a shower looking out onto a courtyard ringed by hedges or opening onto a private balcony is not at all uncommon in a chic contemporary bathroom.

Some bathrooms go further, using glazed doors or fully retractable sections of wall to connect with the world outside. Some even manipulate their floorplans so that shower fittings or tubs are physically located in those exterior spaces. By such means these bathrooms embrace not only the views, but the breezes, scents and sounds of the garden or courtyard, too. The effect is enchanting.

2 Taking its inspiration from Japanese bathing traditions, this spa tub is located outdoors, at the far end of a landscaped bamboo grove. The dense foliage helps to screen the space from view.

2

❶ A eucalyptus-green counter, birch cabinetry and handles made from polished stones are sympathetic partners for the wooded view reflected in the vanity mirror.

❷ The wall above the bath is fully glazed, making the view a fundamental element of the bathroom.

❸ This space is typical of many contemporary bathrooms in that it has been designed to maintain the architectural style of the rest of the house, especially in the way it connects with the outdoors. In this case, the bathroom literally opens up to the world outside via a set of folding doors. The exposed wooden beams and rugged slate flooring have a raw appeal that allows the internal space to blend with the landscape beyond.

❶

❶ Bathrooms that incorporate fully fledged greenhouses aren't all that common, and yet the idea makes perfect sense. After all, the bathroom is made to withstand hot, moist air — just the conditions that are prevalent inside a greenhouse. Here, the blooms can be seen — even smelled — through sliding windows above the bath. A louvered door provides access and promotes air circulation around the two spaces.

❷ Thoughtful design makes the most of the combined room's location on the sunny side of the house. Natural light passes through the fiberglass mesh walls of the greenhouse and again through the sliding windows of the bathroom and then reflects off the stainless steel counters and high-gloss cabinetry.

❶

❶ A few well-chosen accessories give this powder room an aquatic look, in keeping with the nearby living spaces. The bare bones of the space — the horizontal white tiles and the dark jarrah hardwood cabinetry — are not at all suggestive of the sea, so future owners will not be tied to a marine theme.

❷

MARINE BATHROOMS

Even the Romans felt moved to embellish their baths with images of the ocean, rendering pretty and playful fish or cavorting sea monsters in their skillful mosaic work. The wide variety of modern decorative tiles that feature all manner of marine animals — from starfish to dolphins to dreamy mermaids — suggests that the idea of fashioning the family bathroom as a deep-sea paradise is still a popular one.

Aquatic themes are a particular favorite in the decoration of children's bathrooms, where cartoon-like characters can ring the room in the form of border tiles or appear in scattered, handpainted feature tiles across the floor or walls. A more serene, adult version of an ocean-inspired bathroom might see romanticized images of sea horses or dolphins or drifts of shells illustrated in fine mosaic work on the floor of the bathroom or in a feature panel on a wall.

❷ Expanses of mosaic tiling in oceanic blue and a floor set with river stones embellish this beachcombers' bathroom.

❸ Rather than paint a mural directly onto the ceiling, the owners of this bathroom have used a painted canvas hung on stainless steel wires. It's easier for the artist to paint a conventional canvas than to spend several days on ladders or scaffolding working on a ceiling, and it means that the mural can be disassembled should the owners one day decide to sell the house and move on.   ❸

Handpainted murals are an equally evocative way of introducing marine themes to the bathroom. An accomplished mural artist might paint the bathroom ceiling to represent those rippled glimpses of sky and clouds visible from below the waves, suggesting that the bathroom occupies some Atlantis-like space on the sea floor. The great advantage of paint is that it can easily be painted over if the appeal of a marine-themed bathroom begins to fade.

Rather than take inspiration from either natural or mythical marine creatures, some bathrooms pursue a jaunty maritime style. Commonly these bathrooms are decked out in navy and white with perhaps a dash of red or yellow and feature images of yachts, lighthouses, anchors or life buoys, again rendered either in tile work or as murals.

Color offers a less literal way of evoking an oceanic look in the bathroom, all the more so if it is combined with materials used in a sophisticated way. Wrapping the walls and the bath and shower surrounds in languorous shades of blue and green glass mosaic tiles could yield a more sensual deep-sea atmosphere than any number of maritime creatures.

❶ The walls of this small bathroom are clad in teak planking to recreate the ambiance of a ship's cabin. Authentic accessories, including a brass bell, drive home the theme.

❶

❷ Sometimes color alone can be used to create aquatic character in the bathroom. In this instance, tiles the color of the Pacific Ocean bring the glorious sea view beyond the window into the interior. The tiles wrap around the bath and scale the walls to replicate the ocean horizon, further melding the interior and exterior spaces.

❷

❷

❶ The carved and painted wooden grill used to screen the window in this bathroom is evidence of its Southeast Asian influences. Note, too, that the bathroom connects with a nearby pavilion via stepping stones that cross a lush pond.

❷ The exposed nature of this bathroom and the raw textures of the concrete and wicker capture the informality of the tropics and give the space a fresh, modern, organic look.

❸

EASTERN BATHROOMS

Bathing has ritual significance in many Eastern cultures. In countries such as Japan and Korea it is valued not just as a hygienic exercise but as a meditative process. Not surprisingly, the interest in making the home a space for sensory experience has seen a corresponding trend toward Oriental decor in contemporary Western bathrooms.

Some bathrooms strive to faithfully reproduce traditional Eastern bathrooms: Japanese bath houses with their wooden tubs are probably the most popular example of this trend. Others use colors and shapes and perhaps a few authentic accessories to summon up the tropical exuberance of the subcontinent or the lush, garden-style spaces typical of Bali.

❸ An antique Indonesian door was the inspiration for this breezily tropical bathroom. Like the door, the plinth used to support the hand basin is made of teak. The gold faucetry was suggested by the gilded detailing of the door frame. And the door's massive scale is matched by the shape and size of the window at the far end of the bathroom.

The materials chosen for the surfaces of the Eastern-inspired bathroom may make the difference in terms of achieving a space with a genuinely affecting ambiance rather than one that simply looks gimmicky. Steer away from glossy ceramic tiles and instead look for natural stones, pebbles and even concrete.

It's possible to source larger, structural pieces that can be built into the shell of the bathroom. They are likely to be expensive purchases and, because of their non-standard proportions, are even more expensive to install, but richly carved doors, delicate screens and weathered shutters will deeply entrench the character of the bathroom. Another effective but slightly less troublesome strategy is to source furniture pieces, such as tables and chests made in India, Japan or Indonesia, and adapt them for use as vanity cabinets.

❶ This bathroom uses organic materials to create a serene ambiance reminiscent of Japanese interiors. A large bath made from heat-retaining cast iron makes particular reference to the tradition of the Japanese soaking tub.

❷ Sliding doors fitted with horizontal panels of sandblasted glass recall the ethereal translucence of traditional Japanese shoji screens. It's also interesting to note that the architect managed to instill a sense of spaciousness in this tiny bathroom by taking out the existing ceiling to expose the roof trusses and reveal the full height of the roof.

❸ The rich red marble that wraps around this bathroom establishes an exotic Oriental look, which is given emphasis by the carved wooden statue.

VANITIES AND STORAGE

Many people spend more time at the vanity, applying make-up, grooming hair, brushing teeth and washing hands, than soaking in a tub or enjoying a shower. Yet when it comes to bathroom design, vanities often get less attention than those scene-stealing bathtubs and showers. Like any hardworking area, the vanity will benefit from the efficiencies of good design.

VANITIES

A hand basin is essential in a bathroom, but its role can vary with the setting. A modest powder room may be little more than a place for washing hands, while a glamorous dressing room will be the setting for hours of pampering and luxury.

A simple wall-mounted basin, perhaps partnered with a mirror, is a sensible choice in a small bathroom or a separate powder room. These self-contained units can be installed almost anywhere, even in a corner or behind a door. Visually, they have a space-saving impact as they do not take up

PREVIOUS PAGES As the name suggests, the purpose of the vanity is to provide the surface and fixtures required for personal grooming. For some, these needs might be met by something as simple as a hand basin and faucet raised on a plinth. For others, it could mean extensive storage space and a grand, gilt-framed mirror.

❶ The bathroom's identity as a utilitarian room is being replaced by the idea of the bathroom as a retreat in which to spend time pleasurably. Correspondingly, there is new interest in giving bathrooms a more furnished look. Here, a basin sits atop a wooden slab. The combination fulfills the role of a hand basin and vanity counter, yet it has the simple appeal of a porcelain bowl sitting on a tabletop.

❷ A wall-mounted corner basin is the most space-efficient unit available. Of course, it provides no room for storage. If this basin is to be used in a fully functioning bathroom rather than a simple powder room, alternative storage solutions will be required.

❸ The square shape of this wall basin picks up on the graphic quality of the mosaic tiling, a look that is repeated throughout the house. The extended sides serve as counter space, permitting this unit to act as a fully fledged vanity rather than just a hand basin.

floorspace and sightlines are unobstructed right through to the wall on which they are fixed. Plumbing can be installed in the wall or left exposed, an approach that can be appealing if the bathroom has a modern industrial or an eclectic vintage style. Bear in mind that plastic pipes are far less expensive than metal pipes and are therefore usually installed by plumbers as a matter of routine. While this is perfectly satisfactory when the plumbing is concealed, it is probably not the best option when exposed. A decision to use exposed pipes will probably also mean a decision to use more expensive metal pipes.

Pedestal basins are almost as valuable in a small space as wall-mounted basins, though this does not apply to the period models, which tend to have handsome shapes, but bulky dimensions. Modern versions of the pedestal basin are extraordinarily diverse, from futuristic stainless steel to hand-blown glass hand basins.

Setting a basin into a cabinet of some kind means coupling the hand-washing functions of the vanity with some useful storage space. Cantilevered or wall-mounted vanities are increasingly popular, providing storage capacity yet leaving the floor area clear of obstruction. This approach can be very practical, providing foot space in a cramped bathroom, but it can also be employed aesthetically to evoke a visual lightness in minimalist bathrooms or in softly styled, meditative bathrooms featuring pale colors and muted surfaces.

If space is not an issue, the vanity cabinet can certainly be designed to the scale of a grander room. It may stretch from floor to ceiling and wall to wall, with twin basins, huge volumes of storage, built-in lighting and more. Twin basins, championed by those who prefer not to wait while other family members apply their make-up or finish brushing their teeth, are almost mandatory in newly built bathrooms.

❶ This basin was installed in a wet room, a space without shower walls designed to withstand any amount of water. Cabinetry would have been a problem here, but this ceramic pedestal basin is entirely waterproof.

❶

❷ The frame of this vanity, built in a chocolate-toned wood, is a warm but sleek partner for the stainless steel basin.

❸ Storage was an issue in this bathroom, which services three bedrooms. To maximize cabinet space, the designer opted to extend the cantilevered vanity behind the bathtub.

❹ The ledge behind these twin wall-mounted basins conceals the plumbing and forms a long shelf for the storage of toiletries.

❺ The ethereal quality of this pedestal basin is emphasized by the use of a glass hand basin and by the fine lines of the glass shelf and rimmed mirror mounted above.

①

❶ A magnifying mirror and a pair of rails for hand towels have been installed on the wall, leaving this decorative vanity clear of clutter and making the most of its pretty appearance.

A slightly more unusual alternative is the trough-style basin — a long basin overhung by two sets of faucets. In stainless steel or cast concrete these trough basins can look sleek and sophisticated; rendered in chiseled stone they can appear rugged and rustic.

If you're adventurous — and confident of your plumber's skills — you could think about using an unconventional object as a basin. With the right plumbing, anything from an old wash tub to an antique planter pot can be converted into a strikingly original hand basin.

②

❷ These glass basins are set well apart, making it easy for two people to use the bathroom at once.

❸ A blade wall faced with dramatically veined marble separates the vanity area from the bathing area in this bathroom. The trough sink has a strong visual impact and emphasizes the room's rugged ocean outlook.

③

❶ Built as an island unit in the center of a vast bathroom, this central feature incorporates back-to-back vanities.

❷ Some manufacturers have begun to produce decorative ceramic bathroom ware, in line with a growing demand for highly individualistic interiors. It's also possible to source other, unconventional vessels and, with the aid of a skilled plumber, adapt them for use as basins.

❸ Teaming slim cabinets with semi-recessed basins makes the most of wall space in a small bathroom. It also means reduced counter area, but this won't be a problem as long as there are plenty of drawers and cabinets below.

❹ Installed in a small powder room, this unit did not need to incorporate storage space. Taking advantage of this freedom, the owners had the entire vanity, including the basin, carved from a piece of blue marble.

STORAGE

The items that need storing in a bathroom tend to be small: cosmetics, bottles of perfume, medicines, grooming tools such as combs and manicure sets, and perhaps some linens or cleaning products. Almost always, these can be contained in shallow shelves or cabinets. In fact, items stored on broader shelves or in deeper cabinets are likely to be lost or forgotten.

Look to the walls above the bathtub, the basin and the toilet for extra storage space; often these can be fitted with narrow shelves or a slim cabinet, but don't install anything too wide or you'll risk hitting your head with irritating regularity. The wall cavities can be an opportunity for those undertaking new building work — shelves or cabinets can be installed so that they occupy a niche in the wall and don't use up valuable space in the bathroom.

 A small cabinet, which backs into the wall cavity, sits immediately below the vanity mirror, flush with the surrounding tiles. This easily accessible storage bay keeps everyday items such as toothbrushes and lipsticks off the counters, maintaining the room's clean look.

❶

❷

❷ Storage units above the toilet suite make use of an otherwise vacant space.

❸ A long stretch of vanity cabinetry means a welcome abundance of storage space, but it can be visually overwhelming, even in a large bathroom. Here, cantilevered construction allows the cabinetry to sit up off the floor, ensuring that the effect isn't too heavy.

❶

❷

❶ A table-style vanity is a light choice for this small and delicate bathroom. Glass shelves below the basin maintain the look of the piece as furniture, while equipping the unit with much-needed storage space.

❷ Choosing a vanity cabinet for a small bathroom often involves making a choice between storage space and open floorspace. Here a compromise has been reached. The stepped-in units to either side of the central basin provide ample storage without encroaching too much on the floor area.

❸ This piece of cabinetry serves several purposes. Although it looks nothing like the standard vanity cabinet, its location alongside the hand basin means that it is perfectly placed for storing all the paraphernalia of the daily routine. It also has a structural role, acting as a privacy screen for the toilet suite. And it plays a part in the visual style of this bathroom, providing a vertical line of warm wood to contrast with the neighboring horizontal bank of black mosaic tiles.

❹ This shallow, rectangular master bathroom manages to incorporate a considerable amount of storage space, despite its slim dimensions. A vanity runs almost the entire length of the long wall, providing plenty of room for toiletries. The great bonus here is a full-height storage bay, which fills the gap between the shower recess and the outer wall of the bathroom. Remember that towels should only be stored in the bathroom if the space has good ventilation.

16

BATHTUBS

Bathtubs epitomize the pampering potential of the contemporary bathroom. Showers are useful in the morning before you rush out the door, but bathtubs are for long, lazy soaks when the working day is done. Tubs are a place in which to linger, so they must be designed with style, comfort and even outlook in mind.

①

BATHTUBS

Bathtubs are an indulgence in the modern home. They represent the luxury of time, an experience that has little to do with cleansing and everything to do with idle pleasure.

For these reasons, the bathtub is more an object of desire than ever before, and its appearance and performance have become matters of considerable discussion in the planning of the perfect bathroom.

Antique or reproduction claw-foot tubs, a must in a strictly traditional period-style bathroom, have qualities that can be used to advantage in more contemporary settings, too. The footed bathtub has a certain charm that can work to advantage

PREVIOUS PAGES The claw-foot bath is the epitome of romantic bathing for many traditionalists, but a modern, masculine tub can offer an experience every bit as luxurious.

① For some, a sunken bathtub represents the most decadent of bathing experiences. Here, a stainless steel ladder is a practical means of access but it also gives the bath the look of a bijou swimming pool.

② Contemporary versions of freestanding tubs are often an effective choice in a home where traditional touches mingle with the clean lines of modern design.

②

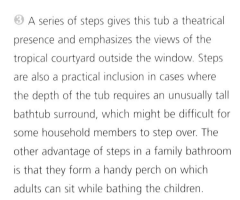

③ A series of steps gives this tub a theatrical presence and emphasizes the views of the tropical courtyard outside the window. Steps are also a practical inclusion in cases where the depth of the tub requires an unusually tall bathtub surround, which might be difficult for some household members to step over. The other advantage of steps in a family bathroom is that they form a handy perch on which adults can sit while bathing the children.

④ Wooden shutters and a paneled bathtub surround give this peaceful bathing area a furnished look, emphasized by comforting additions such as the decorative chair.

③ ④

❶ Locating a tub in a room with awkward dimensions can be a challenge, but there is no point wasting the space between the end of the bathtub and the wall. Here, the bathtub surround has been extended to meet up with the vanity, creating a useful ledge.

❶

❷ The luxurious character of a sunken tub is undermined when it is cramped by heavy cabinetry. The cantilevered construction of this vanity gives the tub that necessary sense of space. Glazing that comes right down to the edge of the bathtub makes the most of the garden view.

in an eclectic setting. For example, a refinished antique tub would combine well with streamlined, shop-bought fittings and decorative pieces of bric-a-brac for a modern cosmopolitan character. Or the bathtub can be pretty and feminine, a perfect choice for a bathroom that evokes a characteristically delicate Parisian style. Because it stands off the floor, the claw-foot tub also has a visual lightness that could suit a whitewashed, wood-bleached, beach-themed bathroom.

Old tubs picked up at secondhand stores or salvaging yards usually require resurfacing. Do-it-yourself resurfacing kits, available at hardware stores or painting specialists, are an inexpensive means of making over an old tub, but the process involves heavy-duty chemicals and can result in a less than perfect finish if instructions are not followed to the letter. Professional resurfacing treatments do cost more, but are certainly less time consuming and probably more reliable. Professional resurfacing can be carried out off site at a commercial workshop or in the bathroom itself.

Tubs designed to be fitted into solid surrounds are usually made of either acrylic or steel. Acrylic tubs are less expensive, and because they are lighter are more readily installed in upper story bathrooms. However, acrylic tubs are less effective at maintaining the heat of the bathwater. The steel versions are more expensive and more heat-efficient, though heavy, which may present challenges during installation. Acrylic tubs can be scratched and therefore stained, while enamel-coated steel tubs are in danger of chipping if heavy objects (such as an electric razor or a bottle of perfume) accidentally fall on the surface.

The surrounds of these fitted bathtubs can be clad with any number of water-resistant materials, from ceramic tiles to treated wooden paneling to stainless steel or river pebbles.

❶ The stone tiles used throughout the
bathroom also clad the interior of this tub,
which was custom made and crafted on site
to make the most of difficult dimensions.

❷

The most common surround is a straight, vertical plane that
matches the line of the tub. It is possible, though, to build
surrounds of any shape. A deep oval surround, for example,
makes a dramatic feature of the tub. Surrounds can also be
extended to fill gaps, creating useful ledges between the ends
of the bathtub and the walls of the bathroom.

Tubs can also be custom made, but this is highly specialized
work and you will need to find an experienced person to do
the job. Usually, the structure is formed with concrete and
then lined with tiles or, in some cases, wood. Custom-made
tubs are usually more expensive than the shop-bought variety,
but can be highly individualistic in appearance.

❷ The trend toward bathing as a pastime is apparent in the
luxurious extras being included in some modern bathrooms.
In some rooms, it's a television; here, it's a warming fire.

❸ Concrete can be colored, sculpted and poured into a
variety of forms to produce a one-of-a-kind bathtub. Its
undeniably rough and rugged character makes concrete
an effective partner of organic materials such as wood.   ❸

17

SHOWERS

Space constraints in contemporary homes, and busy lifestyles, mean that many bathrooms are planned without bathtubs. In such rooms, the shower takes on a more central role in the design. At the same time, the trend toward making the bathroom a space for pampering means that showers are larger and more luxurious than ever.

SHOWERS

The shower will be utilized every day by all members of the household, so there is no point engaging in matters of aesthetics until the issue of functionality has been addressed.

The key requirement is waterproofing. If you opt for a shower fitting installed over a tub, the base of the tub becomes the floor of the shower, a more than adequate arrangement for the run-off of shower water. Splashing water must be contained either by a shower curtain or by a solid fixture, such as a panel of glass that rises from the side of the bathtub to a height above the shower fitting.

Self-contained showers can be bought from a specialist manufacturer and installed in the bathroom, or they can be custom made. Some showers use acrylic or ceramic shower trays as their bases. As long as the join between the shower base and the walls of the shower is well sealed, these should

PREVIOUS PAGES Fashion in contemporary showers runs to two extremes: on the one hand the minimalist wet-room shower, on the other the spacious shower room.

❶ A shower surround of glass bricks allows light from the circular window to reach deep into the interior of the room.

❷ The floor of this shower has been designed and built for good drainage. As a result the floor flows seamlessly from the bathroom's main space into the shower area, maintaining the room's pleasingly clean lines.

❸ Windows above head height bring natural light into the shower area and permit steam to escape the bathroom.

provide a good waterproof floor. Poor-quality acrylic bases have been known to flex and thus undermine their sealed seams. The alternative is to use the floor of the bathroom as the floor of the shower, in which case close attention must be paid to achieve effective drainage. The water should run straight down the drain rather than collecting in pools or, worse, spilling out into the rest of the bathroom or into an adjoining bedroom or hallway. Have no qualms about quizzing the tradespeople involved in the installation of your shower about their experience in getting this crucial matter right first time. Errors can usually only be rectified by demolishing the existing floor and laying a new one.

Custom-made showers can be fashioned from any number of waterproof materials, such as glass bricks, treated wood, corrugated metal sheeting, sandblasted glass or something as conventional and solid as tiled masonry walls. If all the appropriate care and attention are given to waterproofing those surfaces and their seams, such showers can be sublimely harmonious with the rest of the bathroom or vivaciously idiosyncratic in style. The other great advantage of a custom-built model is that it can be sized and shaped to suit the dimensions of the room.

It's also worth noting that walls are not essential to the efficient functioning of a shower. The purpose of containing running, splashing water is to protect the surrounding area from water damage and to reduce the likelihood of a wet and slippery bathroom floor. If the entire bathroom is designed as a wet room, with waterproof surfaces and good drainage, then it is certainly possible to install a shower without the necessity of an enclosure. This is an approach used frequently in minimalist bathrooms, where the aesthetic aim is to keep the space as sparse as possible.

❶ This bathroom has been designed as a wet room, meaning that all surfaces are waterproof. As a result, there is no need to enclose the shower. The marble-clad blade wall shows just how striking a wet-room shower can be.

❷|❸
❹|❺

❶

❷ A panel of glass fixed between the top of the bath and the ceiling is a much more tailored way of containing the shower than the old-fashioned shower curtain.

❸ A completely separate shower room creates a luxurious space for washing and ensures that the rest of the bathroom is kept free of steam and splashes.

❹ Sliding doors open onto an outdoor shower area in this beachside house. The integrated, tile-topped plinth provides a simple shelf for toiletries.

❺ Sliding shower doors built from custom-made glass panels suit the sophisticated city look of this apartment bathroom.

A variation on this idea is the shower room: a space completely waterproofed and fitted with one or more showerheads. Because they operate as a room quite separate from the main body of the bathroom, these are guaranteed to keep splashes away from the vanity and toilet suite. Shower rooms are conducive to shared showers: a luxurious option for couples and a brilliantly playful way for a gaggle of children to scrub up together.

A staggering array of shower fittings is also available. The fixed overhead shower is less popular these days, partly because of its lack of flexibility. It does, however, deliver a soothing downpour of water. Height-adjustable rails are valuable in a family situation, so each family member can alter the position of the showerhead to suit their height. Shower sets with flexible hoses that allow the showerhead to be used in a fixed position or as a hand-held unit also offer versatility. When hand-held, the showerhead is very useful for washing the children's hair, rinsing sand-encrusted feet or giving the family dog a spruce-up.

Water-saving showerheads are readily available. The very best offer a water consumption rate of around 2 gallons (7.5 liters) per minute, although a rate of up to 4 gallons (15 liters) per minute is still an improvement on most older models.

❶ This programmable shower system, incorporating a total of eight spray jets, represents the ultimate in personalized showering comfort.

❷ Twin showerheads and a deep bench seat indicate that this shower room was built as a space in which to spend time comfortably. It's further evidence that showering — and bathing in general —

is seen not just as a functional activity but as a pleasurable experience that makes up part of an individual's leisure time.

❸ Occupying a small nook at one end of a small bathroom, this shower could have looked drab. Instead, a striking pattern, wrapping right around the walls, floor and ceiling, makes it a showpiece.

❷

❸

18

BATHROOM LIGHTING

Lighting is a crucial element of bathroom design. So, too, is privacy. Balancing these two needs doesn't have to mean settling for small windows and allowing electric lighting to do the work. The modern bathroom utilizes both natural and artificial light, making it a pleasant place to be at any time of day or night.

BATHROOM LIGHTING

If the bathroom is to serve as a place of seclusion and sanctuary, then it really needs to be a space that is pleasant to occupy, a space that benefits from the healthful glow of daylight and breathes with the gentle currents of natural breezes. Windows are one of the most effective means of creating such a space, and yet they have the potential to undermine the privacy of the bathroom. Finding a good balance between fresh air, natural light and personal privacy is one of the crucial challenges of bathroom design.

WINDOWS

Despite its new identity as a room for leisure and relaxation, the bathroom is still sometimes a relatively low priority on floorplans. Views, if they are to be had, are more likely to be allotted to a living room or a bedroom, leaving the bathroom to look out over a driveway or an expanse of roof tiles, an aspect which does not need to be maximized. Moreover, there is a reluctance to install large windows, given that they also allow a more extensive view of the interior of the bathroom from outside.

Because of these issues, bathroom windows are often small and frequently filled with patterned or colored glass that obscures views in both directions. The problem with this approach is that it ignores a fundamental role of windows.

PREVIOUS PAGES Materials such as frosted glass panels and glass bricks can be used to let in some natural light while maintaining the privacy of the room. Natural light is highly desirable, but even the sunniest of bathrooms must also contain arrangements of electric light fittings that produce strong, shadowless illumination for all the fine details of personal grooming.

❶ A skylight is an excellent way to bring light into a shower area: privacy is maintained and the ceiling-mounted skylight will capture all the available sunlight.

❶

❷ The lower panels of these doors are frosted, but the upper panels are clear, allowing light from an exterior window to penetrate the space and preserving a sense of the large dimensions of this apartment.

❸ Even when the wooden blind is shut, natural light still pours into this bath area through the glazed ceiling panels above.

❹ Windows set up high on the wall have several advantages: they protect privacy, serve as a light source and contribute to natural ventilation.

❺ When fully open, these frosted glass louvers allow hot, moist air to escape the bathroom. When closed, they let in light without undermining privacy.

If well placed, they can bring natural light into the room and play a vital role in the ventilation process.

Windows placed above head height assure a high level of privacy while still acting as a source of natural light, provided that they are not shaded by awnings on the exterior of the building. High windows can also be used to allow hot air and steam to escape the room.

Windows placed at conventional height and expanses of full-height, floor-to-ceiling glazing can also be utilized in the bathroom, as long as they are well positioned. Slim panels of fixed glass on either side of the vanity, for example, can provide a great bounty of shadowless natural light without necessarily endangering the privacy of the shower or toilet.

Internal shading devices, such as drapes and blinds, can be used to control privacy levels as required. The classic example of this idea is to install a bath in a deep window box with views into the garden or across to a glorious seascape. Shutters controlled from the bath can be closed while the bather steps

❶ This decorative pendant light contributes to the gracious character of the space but it is not relied upon to provide functional lighting. That role is filled by downlights installed flush with the ceiling.

❷ Vertical blinds can be angled so that bathers can enjoy glimpses of the garden while still masking views into the bathroom from outside.

❸ Gentle ambient light is preferable to sharp directional lighting around the tub. This dainty chandelier gives off a soft glow and adds to the feminine atmosphere.

❶

❶ Light fittings set on either side of the mirror result in a shadowless light ideal for detailed tasks, such as shaving or applying make-up.

❷ A well-placed skylight can eliminate the need for artificial lighting throughout the day. Here, the combination of abundant natural light and an all-white color scheme produces a fresh and bright atmosphere.

❸ This vertical strip of louvers is placed in such a way that it does not permit any compromising views of the interior of the bathroom. It does, however, serve as a source of natural light and play a part in the natural ventilation of the room.

into the deep tub, opened once they are submerged in the water, then closed again when it is time to step out.

LIGHTING

Sunshine is a beautiful thing. It provides a soft and flattering light at no cost and without affecting the environment in any negative way. Of course, it must be supplemented by electric, or artificial, lighting.

In the bathroom, artificial lighting falls into two categories. One is commonly called task lighting. This refers to the specific and purposeful illumination of the bathroom's functional areas, particularly the vanity, which is the venue for activities such as shaving or applying make-up. To make these tasks as easy as possible and to limit eye strain, lights around the vanity should be positioned to produce a light that is shadowless. The very best set-up is to install light fittings above the mirror and to either side, an arrangement that tends to produce a fairly uniform level of illumination. The fittings themselves are a matter of taste, from the flamboyant glamour of Broadway dressing room-style bulbs to a discreet installation of strip lights set into the frame of the mirror.

The other category of artificial lighting is called ambient, or mood, lighting, and refers to the general, non-specific illumination of the room. Downlights, wall-mounted uplights or centrally located pendant lights — a must-have in authentic period bathroom refurbishments — can all be usefully applied to suit this purpose. Have them fitted with dimmers so you can enjoy a peaceful soak in the bathtub under a gentle glow.

SKYLIGHTS

Skylights vary enormously in style and function. The simplest can bring an injection of natural light into small, internal bathrooms at a cost of just a few hundred dollars. The most elaborate will cost into the thousands but can offer broad views of perfect blue skies or maybe a patch of stars for moonlit bathing, and boast features such as electrically operated shade devices, a heat-reducing solar blind or an integrated exhaust fan. The advantage of choosing a skylight that can be opened (rather than a fixed skylight), or one that incorporates side vents, is that it can serve a role in the ventilation process as well as acting as a source of natural light.

VENTILATION

Without adequate ventilation, the bathroom soon becomes an unpleasant and even unhealthy place. Ideally, a bathroom space should have ample, big windows that are positioned to promote cross-ventilation and opened after every hot bath

or steamy shower. However, this is rarely the case and would be impractical in cooler climates.

An adaptation of this idea is to install windows with multiple panels that can open separately. Hot air rises, so the top panels can be opened to let the steam out while the main body of the window remains closed, maintaining privacy and keeping the room free of direct breezes. If using windows that are hinged at the bottom of the frame, be sure to have them fitted so that the panel tips out rather than in, encouraging the hot air to flow up and out of the room. Similarly, the blades of louvered windows will need to be angled so that they slant outward and upward. And, as mentioned earlier, skylights that can be opened and those that incorporate side vents allow hot, moist air to escape while also admitting some natural light.

Electric extractor fans mounted on the wall or ceiling can be used as an alternative to natural methods of ventilation, or as a supplementary aid. To maximize the effectiveness of an extractor fan, ensure there is some fresh air coming in to the bathroom to replace the air being extracted. In a bathroom with only a sealed window or skylight, this may mean fitting the internal door with a simple vent.

❶

❶ Here, a pair of windows allows a cross-breeze to clear moist, humid air from the bathroom. Opposite the vanity, a simple blind can be pulled up to maximize the natural light entering through the clear glass window. The window above the bath has frosted glass for permanently reliable privacy.

❷ A skylight that can be opened does double duty, serving as an escape vent for hot, humid air as well as drawing in plenty of natural light to illuminate the bathroom.

❸ In this bathroom, daylight entering through a nearby exterior window provides enough lighting for simple tasks. Downlights mounted above the vanity mirror provide the strong light required for more precise tasks. The louvers can be adjusted to allow a variable flow of air to ventilate the bathroom.

❷

❸

BATHROOM SURFACES

The fundamental requirement of all surface materials is that they are able to withstand the warm, moist environment of the bathroom — and yet they contribute so much more. Survey your options and then choose the surface materials that will bring the desired textures, colors and atmosphere to your bathroom.

BATHROOM SURFACES

These days, bathrooms are rooms in which to linger, escaping the hustle of the household or recuperating from the stresses of the working day. Accordingly, the design and decoration of the bathroom is now given as much focus as in other rooms.

Paint, which serves as such an effective color tool elsewhere in the house, is not as prominent in the bathroom, where issues of water resistance are a crucial consideration. Instead, color is featured through the use of various materials, from tile and classic stone to sleek modern steel and glass. When selecting bathroom surfaces, be aware that they serve a decorative as well as a functional purpose. Be prepared to mix and match materials, too. Take the confidence you have used to decorate other rooms in the house and use it to match pale limestone walls with a glazed eggplant floor tile and a striking piece of chartreuse-green cabinetry.

WOOD

The remarkable variation in tone and pattern from species to species means that wood has the aesthetic qualities to serve any style of bathroom. Warm and friendly, a simple honeyed pine suits the uncomplicated charms of a country cottage bathroom. In a grand old house, a richly toned wood can bring to the bathroom all the brooding luster of the period. Oak picks up the decorative theme of an Arts and Crafts period interior, beech on the icy restraint of Scandinavian design, black-stained wood on the bohemian drama of an early 20th-century glamour.

PREVIOUS PAGES The materials used to clad and protect surfaces in the bathroom also contribute elements of color, texture and pattern.

❶ Wood is a familiar element in the domestic context and can be used to make the bathroom feel comfortable and livable. In this space, a wooden slab supports a pair of basins: it's a modern take on the vintage look of a bowl atop a freestanding table.

❶

| ❷ | ❸ |
| ❹ | ❺ |

❷ The tiger-stripe grain of the teak cabinetry has an almost graphic impact in this Balinese-inspired bathroom. Teak — a very heavy, hard wood — was chosen because it is commonly used for furniture in Indonesia.

❸ Sealed wood is reasonably reliable as a vertical surface, but less so as a horizontal surface. Here the ship-shape horizontal teak paneling of the vanity cabinets is topped with a limestone counter.

❹ A copper plinth is topped with a circular jarrah hardwood counter to support a basin.

❺ Here, wood clads a vertical storage unit. This upright dash of dark-toned wood balances the squat expanse of glossy black tiles, making this a visually stimulating space.

❶ A veneer of jarrah hardwood clads the wall from which a toilet is hung. Protected from the shower area by a wall of glass and set well away from any other source of running water, this handsome veneer is in no danger of water damage.

❶

❷ Contrasting materials can be used to give visual definition to different sections of the bathroom, in line with the contemporary trend toward designing the space as a series of functional zones. Here, the wooden surround of the bathtub presents a softer and more leisurely look than the crisp mosaic tiles used in the shower area.

❷

It must be remembered, though, that wood doesn't necessarily fare well in the hot, humid environment of some bathrooms. Wooden cabinetry is less in danger of being adversely affected by the moist conditions, but any surfaces that are directly exposed to water — vanity counters, for example, or floors that lie directly alongside showers and bathtubs — are highly susceptible to damage.

Wooden floors can be used with confidence in a powder room, but if they are to be laid around a bathtub or shower they should be finished to a standard that ensures they can withstand prolonged exposure to water. Certain hardwood species are less susceptible to water damage. One reliable option is to have the floorboards caulked in the style of a ship's deck: the bonding substance that seals the joints between neighboring boards prevents the penetration of water and the resulting stripes produce a nautical look that can be used to advantage.

Another option is to install duckboard as part or all of the bathroom flooring. Historically, duckboard was a boardwalk of wooden slats laid across muddy ground. In the modern bathroom, the term is used to describe the wooden flooring slats set above a conventional waterproof surface, such as a tiled floor. The duckboard adds the warm look and feel of wood, while the spacing between the boards allows water to drip through onto the waterproof surface and flow away through hidden drains. Duckboard is especially popular as a shower floor.

All wood must be properly cured before it is installed; unscrupulous businesses will use "green" timber rather than take the time to let the wood dry properly. Wood that hasn't been cured is likely to shrink, warp or crack. All wooden surfaces should be sealed to prevent water penetration;

oil-based sealers are preferable, and should be reapplied every couple of years.

SOLID SURFACES

Solid surfaces made by blending natural minerals into acrylic or resin are produced by a number of manufacturers and tend to be marketed under their brand names, such as Corian.

The range of standard, solid colors is enormous, so finding a tone to match a much-loved feature tile or to tie in with a nearby bedroom carpet is a relatively easy task. Others are made to look like granite or other natural stones. Interestingly, these man-made stone look-alikes are not necessarily cheaper than the real thing, but they can be molded or milled into just about any form, allowing a level of design freedom not always achievable with the authentic material.

Solid surfaces are non-porous and thoroughly resistant to water damage. They can suffer scratches, but, because the color is solid throughout the material, the affected areas can be lightly buffed to eliminate the damage.

STONE

As delicate as a sun-bleached seashell or as dramatically patterned as a stormy sky, marble has been a favorite in bathrooms for centuries. It is a simply beautiful stone, capable of bringing grandeur to a classical bathroom or a sense of old-world elegance to a quirky, vintage-styled space. The process of vein-matching adjacent slabs of marble to give the impression of an ongoing pattern across the plane of the wall or floor can have a rich and exotic impact if well executed. Though white marble is possibly the most popular, the stone also comes in

❶

① Limestone's popularity parallels the current fashion for low-key and minimalist interiors. Shades of cream are common, but it also comes in pale pinks, golds and darker colors.

② Stone is often associated with looks that are either very severe or very glamorous, but it can also convey something pretty and delicate. That is the case here, where bands of marble mosaic crisscross limestone tiling.

③ There's no doubting marble's credentials as a surface material: it has been used inside and outside buildings for millennia. That proven quality makes it a highly desirable material, but it is also valued for its aesthetic adaptability. Here, it looks masculine and formal. In another context it might look glossy and glamorous or grand and ancient in the manner of a Roman bath.

②

③

succulent caramels, ruddy roses, mossy greens and stormy grays, all of which can be used to great effect.

High-gloss polished marble and matte-finish honed marble both work well as vanity countertops or on vertical surfaces such as walls and bath surrounds. Polished marble can pose a problem when used for flooring as the shiny finish makes for an extremely slippery surface. Sealers that minimize this problem are available, but some have a tendency to give the surface a yellowish tint: ask your supplier for more information on their product before proceeding.

Tumbled marble tiles are made by tumbling the stone with gritty sand and various chemicals to produce a softened, aged texture. It can be used on any bathroom surface, including the floor, but it is far more porous than the untreated stone and therefore must be treated with a sealer to prevent staining. The tumbling process turns a reasonably expensive stone into a very expensive stone, so tumbled marble tiles are often used sparingly in the bathroom, for example as a border to a plain terra-cotta tile floor or as a rustic feature tile on a simple white tiled wall.

Granite is a handsome stone, varying in color from gray to green to dark red and black. Most granite has a very fine flecking through it, but ultimately it serves as a color block in the overall scheme, rather than contributing an element of pattern in the way that a highly decorative marble can. Granite is an inert material, highly resistant to water damage, staining, heat and scratches. It is, however, extremely heavy and may not be viable as flooring for an upstairs bathroom.

Slate has had periods of popularity in the bathroom. Like both marble and granite, it is available in a variety of tones, including gray, green, red, brown, purple and charcoal black. It differs from its grander cousins, however, by being

❸

considerably less expensive. It is porous and both vertical and horizontal slate surfaces require sealing. Slate tiles with a smooth surface finish are available, but a textured surface that suggests a rough-hewn stone is perhaps the most familiar treatment on bathroom floors.

Although it is possible to source pieces of limestone that are as dark as a gray or a mossy green, by far the most popular tones are the pale shades: alabaster white, mild khaki, seashell pink and honey. There is very little variation in color within each piece and its tonal consistency makes it a favorite in minimalist bathrooms, where simplicity is the dominant aesthetic. The density of the stone differs according to its

❶ Like the stone-washing process used on denim, the tumbling treatment of marble produces a soft, aged look and texture. Tumbled marble has a timelessness often used to advantage in classically styled spaces.

❷ This display of slate tiling across walls and floor demonstrates the stone's surprisingly varied color range — gray, pink, purple and auburn all mingle in this bathroom.

❸ A broad marble floor is a sumptuous treatment for a decidedly lavish bathroom. The grandeur of the tiles is given some spark by the bronzed glass mosaic tiles used to clad the outside of the shower.

❶ Bathrooms that are light, bright and breezy in character are very much the dominant trend, but there is also considerable appeal in a bathroom that has the atmosphere of a secret grotto. Here, an unusually dark green limestone has been used to create the mood of a shaded watering hole.

❷ Granite can vary in color from light gray and beige to charcoal and black and is usually densely patterned with fine tonal flecks. The stone's literal and visual weight is sometimes in need of lightening. In this instance, slim steel supports have been used to lift the counter up off the cabinetry, giving the piece a lighter look.

❸ These large wall and floor tiles demonstrate the diversity of veining and coloration in marble. Here, shades of cream, gold, gray and terra cotta are blended into an unusually broad veining pattern.

❷

❸

❶

origin. Some limestones, while suitable for wall applications, are too soft for use on the floor. Those that derive from France or Italy are considered hard enough for floor applications in domestic settings.

TERRAZZO

Terrazzo is a wonderful hybrid product that has something of the stature of a stone floor, but in a range of looks that embraces the warm, classic and whimsical. The material is made by strewing an aggregate material through a concrete base. Conventionally, the concrete is mixed with marble chips, but the modern version of the product has used some interesting aggregates, including shells, colored glass and fragments of brass or copper. The aggregate varies in size from seed-sized granules to pebble-sized chunks. The product can be customized further by adding tints to the concrete base. Terrazzo can be poured in situ or laid as slabs or tiles.

CONCRETE

Concrete has been reborn as a design material in recent years. Raw concrete slab floors, so common in modern homes, can be polished to a luminous, stylish and edgily sophisticated finish or overlaid with a tinted screed, then buffed and sealed. Giving a polished finish to a raw floor is a reasonably inexpensive treatment, but tinted screeds or screeds that incorporate decorative particles, terrazzo-style, can be more expensive. A concrete floor is naturally porous, so must be appropriately sealed.

Concrete is also gaining favor as a material for vanity counters, partly for its industrial look and partly because of the design flexibility it offers. It can be poured into virtually any shape and can be molded to incorporate integrated basins, a seamless look that many find appealing.

❶ Traditionally, terrazzo is made by strewing marble chips through a concrete base. This, however, is an example of a modern terrazzo, with pieces of bottle-green glass providing a link to the glass mosaic wall.

❶

❷ Concrete has a raw, industrial character, but it also partners well with natural materials such as stone and wood. Here, its dual personality is explored in a bathroom that expresses a warmer, more organic version of pared-back minimalism.

❷

❷ Halogen lamps are angled to illuminate this feature wall of marble mosaic tiles, enhancing the soft luster of the tiles and emphasizing subtle variations in color across the surface.

❷

TILES

Glazed ceramic tiles have the advantage of being both attractive and overwhelmingly practical in the bathroom, as they are hard-wearing, water-resistant, mold-resistant and easy to wipe clean. The porous grout between the tiles can attract mold: if you are reluctant to take on the chore of regular brushing, you can enquire about special mold-resistant grouting materials or have the entire tiled surface sealed, including the grout.

It's also possible to tint the grouting material, a strategy that can camouflage slight mold problems but which can also be used to decorative effect, for example by pairing a simple and inexpensive white tile with a black or red grout.

An alternative to the glazed ceramic tile is the fully vitrified tile, which is often used to recreate the aura of 19th- and early

❸ Paint is the very cheapest way to introduce color to a room, but simple ceramic tiling — which has greater water resistance and is therefore of more use in the bathroom — runs a close second. Here, a straightforward checkerboard of blue and white tiles has a bold, graphic effect and helps to camouflage some of the angularity of this small space.

❸

20th-century interiors. The color is constant right through a fully-vitrified tile, so chips and scratches tend to go unnoticed.

Terra-cotta tiles are hand- or machine-cut tiles of baked clay. They have a soft and earthy look, and tend to be comfortingly warm underfoot. They are, however, extremely porous — the paler the tile, the greater the porosity — and must be sealed for use in the bathroom. Some sealers will darken the color of the natural tile.

Mosaic tiling can be an expensive exercise because of the labor involved in laying the tiles. Mosaics can be simple, incorporating, for example, a classic Greek border pattern, or romantically elaborate, featuring seascapes, cherubs or a stylized scene from a Shakespearean play. They can be created using ethereal glass tiles, colorful ceramic tiles or genuine river stones. Aesthetic considerations aside, one of the great advantages of mosaic tiling is that it can follow the contours of a curved surface, such as a rounded bath surround, something larger tiles cannot do. As long as it has been appropriately installed, a mosaic tile floor should last as long as any ceramic tile floor.

Virtually any tile can be used on the walls of the bathroom, or on bath and shower surrounds, but there are some tiles that are not practical for use on the floor. Obviously these include three-dimensional tiles and fragile glass tiles. Highly glazed ceramic tiles should also be excluded from floor applications: the high-gloss surface will make the floor dangerously slippery. Fully vitrified tiles and tiles with a matte glaze do not get slippery when wet and are therefore suitable for use on the bathroom floor.

❶

❶ Ceramic tiles are invested with all the ambiance of their origins. For example, hand-painted, hand-cut tiles from Portugal or Spain have the flamboyance of the sun-soaked Mediterranean. In this instance, horizontally aligned rectangular tiles, commonly used in Victorian-era interiors, immediately convey a sense of tradition. They are updated, however, by the use of a contrasting colored grout.

❷ Intricate mosaics that illustrate classical scenes or whimsical fantasy-scapes are probably best left to the professionals, but a large-scale mosaic made with big pieces of broken tiles is something most enthusiastic amateurs could tackle successfully.

❸ Standard-sized tiles in ravishing colors, such as this vivid lavender, bring oodles of personality to a room at very little cost.

❷

❸

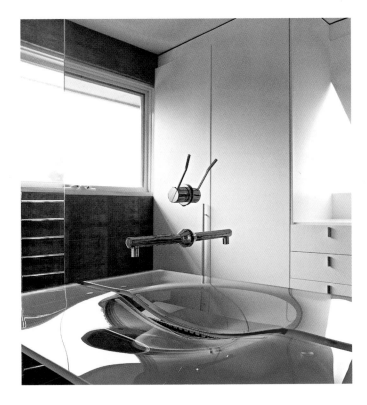

GLASS

Safety glass offers a smooth, sheer surface, very much at home in modern minimalist or industrial-style bathrooms. Clear glass fixed onto a white wall surface will take on a slightly green hue, but you also have the option of painting the back of the glass in the color of your choice. Having the glass back-painted means that you can choose whether the glass blends in seamlessly with the wall color or makes a dramatic and expressive contrast.

Sheets of safety glass should be installed by experienced tradespeople; they will fix the panels to the wall without cracking or chipping the material and apply a sealer around the edges to ensure that no moisture seeps in between the wall and the glass. Glass tiles tend to be simpler to install. Glass mosaic tiles, for example, can even be laid across curved surfaces, lending a bewitching transparency to a circular tub surround. Thick panels of safety glass can also be fashioned into counters.

❶ Ocean-tossed bottles washed up on a beach were the inspiration for this bathroom. The sandy tone was provided by wooden cabinetry, but the sea-washed glass was represented by decorative glass panels and tiles. The glass has been sand-etched to produce a finely textured surface and backpainted with a celadon green.

❷ Glass can be a surprisingly durable surface. Here, a toughened glass counter has been shaped to incorporate a basin.

❸ A frosted glass basin, a clear glass counter and a highly reflective black granite wall provide sparkle in this tiny powder room.

❶ The reflective qualities of glass can be utilized in the bathroom. Here, sunlight bounces off a wall clad in milky glass tiles, making the space feel fresh and airy and tempering the room's decorative austerity with a little softness.

❷ This seaside bathroom was specifically designed to draw in the natural light and catch the ocean breezes. Glass surfaces simply enhance the sensuality of that light and breezy look.

❶

❷

❸

❸ Multicolored glass tiles give a sense of animation to an essentially boxy shower space. Changing the angle of the tiles from diagonal on the floor to vertical on the walls makes clear the definition between the two surfaces. Without that alteration, the treatment would have produced a dizzying optical illusion.

❹ Glass tiles frame the vanity, fulfilling a decorative as well as a functional purpose. Their transparency makes a strong contrast with the heavy stone counter.

❹

❶

① An integrated sink ensures that there are no seams to undermine stainless steel's reputation as an irreproachably hygienic and waterproof surface material.

② Stainless steel on shower walls and the bath surround give this bathroom a quirky, modern and super-clean look.

STAINLESS STEEL

The price of stainless steel has dropped in the last decade or so, bringing it into line with other premium materials, such as granite and marble, and making it an option in domestic bathrooms as a vanity surface or even as a wall cladding. Stainless steel is water-resistant, extremely durable and highly unlikely to stain, but it is prone to surface smears, which can be very difficult to remove. Using a brushed or satin finish eliminates the problem, masking the smudgy fingerprints and camouflaging light scratches. It is possible to have stainless steel countertops custom made to incorporate basins.

③ Stainless steel is one of the most expensive surface materials. However, it comes in sheet form and can be quickly and easily installed, a valuable quality in a project in which glaziers, tilers, plumbers and electricians must be juggled. The same applies to rubber, a material more commonly used on floors. Here, it is used as wall cladding.

LAMINATE

Offering a vast range of colors and patterns and a satisfactory performance at an affordable price, laminates are a long-time favorite for use on vanity cabinets and counters. These days, the material can be curved to incorporate backsplashes, eliminating the join between the vertical and horizontal surfaces and thereby reducing the risk of water damage. Laminate does lack the durability of materials such as stainless steel or granite, but it also costs considerably less. Laminates can also bring a lot of color and individuality to a bathroom: think about using contrasting colors on alternate door panels or selecting something like a chocolate brown laminate for cabinetry below the counter and ice blue for the shelves above.

PAINT

Paint represents an enormously economical wall treatment in the bathroom. A painted wall is not water-resistant in the manner of, for example, steel, glass or glazed tiles, and surfaces that are frequently exposed to splashes should be protected by one of these more water-repellent materials. Away from those areas, however, a gloss or semi-gloss paint makes a perfectly acceptable and affordable wall treatment. Some manufacturers produce bathroom-specific paints that include anti-fungal additives to inhibit mold growth. It's also possible to ask for these additives to be added to standard paint.

❶ This vanity illustrates the creative potential of laminates. Not only does the design exploit the contrasts between the two colored and patterned laminates, it also shows how the material can be coaxed around gentle curves.

❶

❷

❷ Painted surfaces located close to a shower recess or bath are likely to attract mold and mildew, but in areas less affected by warm, moist conditions, they fare well.

❸ Laminates, plain ceramic tiles and paint are all capable of contributing a lot of color and character to a bathroom at a low price. ❸

SUITES

Separately, the peaceful bedroom and the pampering bathroom are the essential luxuries of the contemporary home. Together, they form a private hideaway, a space set apart purely for the deeply therapeutic purpose of rejuvenating body and soul. The perfect suite must indeed be an item on every homeowner's wish list.

SUITES

Partnering a bedroom with a master bathroom to create the ultimate suite makes it possible to indulge in the sensual pleasures of bathing, grooming, resting and sleeping, all in total privacy. It's important to concede that this is a luxury made possible by floorspace and budget: trying to build and furnish a suite with inadequate resources will only lead to disappointment. If neither the floor area nor the finances are available for a truly comfortable master bathroom, then surrender the idea and instead look at building a compact dressing room or a tiny sitting area or simply increasing the size of the whole bedroom.

Bedroom-bathroom combinations work best when there is some degree of separation between the two spaces: the last thing you want when you lie down to read at night is to be

PREVIOUS PAGES A sense of continuity is highly desirable in bedroom-bathroom partnerships. Flooring can be used to unite the two spaces, either by using one material in a single sweep through both rooms or by maintaining a color cue from a tiled to a carpeted floor.

❶ These Japanese shoji panels screen the bathroom while permitting some of the bedroom's natural light to shine through.

❷ The traditional style of the bedroom furnishings is matched by the handsome cherry wood cabinetry in this bathroom.

❸ Here, a broad opening is fitted with doors that slide back into the wall. The result is a clean finish and an enhanced sense of space.

staring at a toilet located too close to your bedside table. Think about where you are likely to position the bedroom furniture and try to organize it so that the bathroom door is located at some distance from the headboard. Also try to avoid locating the bed against the common wall if that is where the plumbing is: the resulting noise can be a disturbance when trying to sleep.

The opposite approach is to have no separation whatsoever between the two spaces, embracing the whole as one unified retreat. An abundance of space is the most important element if this strategy is to succeed, closely followed by impeccable building work that ensures water, heat and steam all stay within the functioning bathroom zone and don't enter the sleeping area.

The idea of matching a master bathroom to a bedroom can be hard to conceptualize at first: one room is a place of tiles, glass and faucets, the other a space of soft carpets and rugs, breezy curtains and comfortable bed linen. The easiest way to achieve a visual connection is to use color. Start by matching the two shells: for example, team up biscuit-toned sisal flooring and a pale parchment paint color in the bedroom with a honey-flecked terrazzo floor and a creamy mosaic wall tile in the bathroom. Then look at the bedroom furnishings and see if you can tie them in with the bathroom fixtures. For example, a country pine bed might suggest a pine or pine-veneer vanity cabinet. A headboard upholstered in ruby micro suede could be the color cue for accent tiles on the bathroom walls.

Look at the physical qualities of the materials, too, and if possible find a way of representing those characteristics in each of the rooms. For example, sheer blinds or drapes

❶

❶ Master bathroom floors must be well constructed to avoid an overflow of water into an adjacent bedroom, particularly if that space is carpeted.

❷ This bathroom maintains a strong connection with its bedroom not by copying its look but by subverting it. The bedroom is enveloped in dusky charcoal tones, while the bathroom is vivid, white and light. The switch in mood occurs right at the border, where the stained wood of the bedroom floor changes to gleaming white marble. It's the clearly defined contrasts between these two spaces that makes them work as a dynamic pair.

❸ Glass panels maintain the sightlines between the bedroom and the bathroom in this quirky modern suite.

❷

❸

① Pieces from the owners' extensive art collection are displayed not only in the bedroom but in the adjacent bathroom, too.

② Feature tiles have been used to create an elegant border at picture-rail height in this bathroom, a detail that ties in with the classic cornices and architraves of the bedroom in this refurbished house.

②

in the bedroom might be balanced by the presence of a luminous glass backsplash behind the hand basin. If the bedroom furnishings all have the mellow gleam of beloved market finds and treasured family heirlooms, then avoid full gloss tiles in the bathroom, and instead look for tiles with a matte finish. You might also substitute something like an antique wall-hung mirror for the frameless mirror panels installed above most modern vanities.

A floorplan that functions well is particularly important in the master bathroom, partly because it is usually a small space, facing all the usual challenges of a diminutively sized bathroom, and partly because any errors related to plumbing and drainage can cause considerable damage to the adjacent bedroom. As usual, the best advice for small-space planning is to be selective. Don't try to cram a full-size bath, a double

③ Colors and shapes are repeated throughout this suite. The warm gray of the bedroom walls and carpet is clearly matched in the tiles that surround the tub and clad the bathroom walls. Another link is provided by the horizontal niche that runs across above the bed, which is balanced by the long, low panel of glazing at the edge of the bath. ③

❶ This suite was built without any structural division between the sleeping space and the bathing space. As a result, both areas can enjoy the views and the abundant natural light afforded by glazing that reaches right to the roofline.

❶

❷ The vanities that flank the entrance to this bathroom look like freestanding cabinets, a strategy that helps to give the combined space the aura of a comprehensively furnished suite. The bathtub, its presence enhanced by a dramatic stone surround, also has the status of a piece of furniture and serves as a counterpoint to the bed, fortifying this suite's very pleasing sense of symmetry.

❷

shower, a toilet suite and a capacious vanity into a space the size of a large pantry: the result will be a room that looks poky and performs poorly. Instead, consider your options and your priorities and then include only those fittings for which you genuinely have space. Fitting a hinged door that swings out into the bedroom rather than into the bathroom itself will create a bit of extra space in the bathroom. A sliding door has similar space-creating advantages, with the additional benefit that it does not impose itself on the floor area of the bedroom either. Best of all the options, perhaps, is a door that slides back into the wall cavity, leaving you free to maximize wall space and floor area in both rooms.

Problems such as water seeping through the walls of the bathroom into a built-in wardrobe or flooding the bedroom carpet are not only irritating and disruptive but can be quite expensive to rectify. Inadequate ventilation systems that result in a humid bedroom are likewise unacceptable.

Before going ahead with any work, ask your prospective tradespeople if they have done similar jobs in the past and if you can speak to some previous clients for a recommendation. Assuming you proceed with the job and are happy with the results, make sure that you offer to serve as a referee for those tradespeople in the future.

TROPICAL OASIS

The super-stylish resorts of modern Asia were the inspiration for this sophisticated suite. Like those chic establishments, the space combines some of the key aspects of traditional Southeast Asian style with the clean, fresh, streamlined look of contemporary minimalism. It's a combination that benefits both aesthetics, lightening the heavy excesses of the tropical look and breathing life into the sometimes cold and characterless tone of minimalist interiors.

The division between spaces is marked not by a wall but by a change in flooring materials, from the wood of the bedroom to the marble of the bathroom. A large double shower spans the wall at the far end of the bathroom, but its frameless glass screen minimizes its impact, maintaining the sense of space and light. The use of a freestanding tub and exposed bath plumbing also contribute to the room's breezy ambiance.

Exposing the bathroom to the bedroom in this way can only succeed if the bathroom is worthy of the attention. Its aesthetic qualities must be very high indeed, and the more mundane aspects of the room's function must be masked or concealed. Here, the toilet is contained in a separate room accessed by a door next to the shower.

❶ The cabinet is made of teak, a wood used commonly in Indonesia. The mirror, too, makes reference to traditional style, its silver and gold leaf patterning recalling the gilded frames of Balinese doors and windows.

❶

❷ The battening of the ceiling is a contemporary take on traditional Southeast Asian architecture. Without the battens, this might look like just another hotel-style bathroom, but their presence makes a connection with the balmy mood of modern tropical interiors.   ❷

① The gold wax finish of the wall behind the headboard gives this suite a sense of occasion.

② Frosted glass walls contain the splashes from the bath and allow some penetration of natural light from the bedroom windows into the interior of the bathroom. They also provide a privacy screen while minimizing the sense of separation between the two spaces.

②

LITTLE BOX OF TRICKS

The strategy employed throughout the apartment in which this suite is located was to create private zones without compromising the spacious, open-plan design of the interior. Here, the only structural elements separating the bathroom from the bedroom are the full-height glass walls above the bathtub and the short wall that forms one side of the shower. The paneled wood used on the bedroom side of the shower wall and the bath surround matches the treatment given to walls and wardrobes elsewhere, masking the bathroom's identity as a functional space. The broad entrance created by the space left between the bath and the shower helps to maintain the open-plan character of the suite.

③ Given its lack of solid structural boundaries, this bathroom needed a strong focal point to draw the disparate fittings and fixtures into a cohesive whole. The vanity area fulfills that role with the dramatic juxtaposition of dark marble wall tiles, a white marble counter and the pale limestone of the floor. ③

TAILOR MADE

A palette of warm neutrals drifts across from bedroom to bathroom in this suite of understated sophistication. In the bedroom, a mushroom-toned carpet is paired with parchment-colored walls, while the bathroom combines earthy ceramic floor tiles and custom-tinted concrete blocks. The furnishings, too, are consistent across the two rooms. Where the bedroom mixes mid-toned wood with soft furnishings in shades of taupe and slate, the bathroom teams its mid-toned wood with gray granite around the tub and on the vanities.

In this suite the bathroom is as spacious as the bedroom, so it was important that both spaces had a similarly strong sense of composition. The massive granite surround of the bathtub gives the tub visual weight, making it as dominant in the bathroom as the tailored bed is in the bedroom.

❶ A full-height panel of glass was installed at the far end of the bathroom to draw in natural light and give the space a connection with the garden outside. A portion of the glass has been frosted as a privacy measure. The frosted finish is repeated as a border around the vanity mirrors and is also used in the wood-framed glass door connecting the bathroom with the bedroom.

❷ Simple forms, neat finishes and a subdued palette unite the two spaces.

❸ A custom-made shower crafted from tinted concrete blocks made it possible to match not only the color of the walls but the curve of the vanities.

A Grand Plan

Working within the restrictions of a heritage-listed house can be challenging, especially when it comes to implementing modern concepts such as master bathrooms. Here, the bathroom was installed in a neighboring bedroom. Original details, including French doors and marble fireplaces, were retained in both rooms. The new tiled surfaces required in the wet zone of the bathroom utilize traditional materials, specifically the hexagonal floor tiles and the bevel-edged tiles of the walls. Fixtures, including the vanity counters and the blade wall that separates bath and vanities from toilet and shower, are rendered in marble, thus bringing the old fireplace into the embrace of the new room. Ultimately, the fireplace and the French doors give this bathroom more charm than could ever be achieved in a brand-new space.

❶ A sleek, freestanding bathtub recalls the shape of traditional claw-foot tubs, and its commanding position in front of the fireplace creates a relationship between the old and the new. The tub rests on top of wooden slats set over a stainless steel tray. Splashes fall through into the tray and drain away. The treatment extends under the marble-clad blade wall and into the shower area behind.

❷ Storage is concealed in the wall space behind the vanity mirrors, reducing the visual distractions and helping to maintain the mood of old-fashioned elegance.

❸ Rich tones of ruby and saffron summon up the grandeur of the room's Victorian heritage.

ROCK SOLID

The use of a blade wall to define the various zones of a suite is common practice in contemporary design. Usually, though, the wall is a solid structure clad in tiles or stone. In this idiosyncratic suite a large boulder is used to screen the bathing areas from the bedroom. The rocky theme, taken from the magnificent landscape of the area in which the house is located, is continued through to the pebbled shower floor and to the rocks that surround the bath, serving as steps into the tub. Aside from the boulder, there is no physical separation between the sleeping and bathing zones of the suite. The sense of unity is enhanced by the use of free-standing vanity cabinets styled to match the authentic Asian furnishings used throughout the house.

❶ This suite's showpiece, a boulder 7 feet high (3 meters high), was craned onto the site and set into a bed of sand and gravel before the house's concrete slab was poured.

❷ Both the bathing and sleeping areas take advantage of an expansive harbor view. Indeed this suite extends beyond its four walls, the glazed doors by the bed leading to a private balcony complete with spa tub.

❸ This most unusual shower is made possible by a stainless steel column, which houses all the plumbing. The column plays a discreet functional role while the pebbles, rocks and indoor tree create the illusion of a natural watering hole.

❶ Ornamental brass pulls and hinges give the vanity cabinets a distinctly Oriental appeal.

❷ The ornamental boulder is the only structure that breaks up the open flow of space from the sleeping area into the bathroom area. As a result, each zone visually draws on the other's volume, making both spaces feel larger than they really are.

❸ Travertine floor tiles and a tumbled marble bath surround have the raw, stony qualities to match the rugged character of the boulder. At the same time, they have a sweet and subtle tone that works well with the light coloring of the bedroom's carpet, wall treatments and soft furnishings.

❶

❷

❸

① When closed, the frosted glass shutters provide a high degree of privacy. When open they permit glimpses of the park view enjoyed from the dressing room windows.

①

② Much attention was paid to the matter of ensuring perfect ventilation in the bathroom. An exhaust system prevents hot, moist air from drifting into the bedroom when the bathroom is in use. Small windows above the bath also help to encourage air flow around the area, even when no steam is being produced.

②

CLASSIC COMPOSITION

Though rooms of generous proportion are usually seen as desirable, they are not always as welcoming, functional and visually appealing as a collection of smaller spaces.

Here, a clever floorplan makes the most of a large area, dividing the space into three: a bedroom, a bathroom and a dressing room. Both the bedroom and the dressing room look out over a park, but while the bathroom has a set of windows for ventilation it has no view of its own. A shuttered internal window in the wall above the bath lets the bathroom enjoy the light and the views from the dressing room's parkside window.

The monochromatic color scheme is carried through from the carpeted floor and painted walls of the bedroom into the limestone tiles of the bathroom's floor and walls. The simplicity of the palette is enlivened by the subtle use of warm textures throughout both spaces. A suede headboard and chenille bedspread are sensual choices in the bedroom, while in the bathroom honed limestone is more tactile than the conventional polished finish.

INDEX

CREDITS

1 Interior designer: Darryl Gordon Design; Photographer: Simon Kenny

2–3 Architect and interior designer: Edgard Pirrotta Architects; Photographer: Shania Shegedyn

4–5 Architect: Sarah Shand; Interior designer: Issenbel.com and Jillian Friedlander; Photographer: Kallan MacLeod

6–7 Interior designer: Elaine Roberts—Homeworks; Photographer: Kallan MacLeod

8 (left) Architect: Hal Walter Architect; Bathroom designer: Geoff Cosier; Photographer: Shania Shegedyn; (right) Architect: John Brooks; Interior designer: Abby Smith, Egan Design; Photographer: Tim Maloney

9 Designer: Glenn Holmes, Design Department; Photographer: Simon Kenny

10–11 Top row (left) Interior designer and art consultant: Lenore West; Architect: Pat Jeffares; Photographer: Kallan MacLeod; (center) Architect: David Luck; Photographer: Shania Shegedyn; (right) Designer: Walter Herman, Ros Palmer Interiors; Photographer: Simon Kenny. Middle row (left) Architect: Hal Walters Architect; Bathroom Designer: Geoff Cosier; Photographer: Shania Shegedyn; (center) Architect: Jackson Clements Burrows; Interior designers: Jackson Clements Burrows and Cardamone Design and owner; Photographer: Shania Shegedyn; (right) Photograph courtesy of Imperial Home Décor Group. Bottom row (left) Designer: Melanie Stewart, Interior Design Company; Photographer: Bruce Nicholson; (center) Architect: HDA Architects; Concept and interior design: IIDA International Design; Photographer: Tim Nolan; (right) Architect: Murray Wood and Jeff Karskens,

Tectonic Developments; Photographer: Simon Kenny

12–13 (1) Architect: Gabriel Poole, Gabriel & Elizabeth Poole Design Co.; Photographer: David Sandison; (2) Architect: Gabriel & Elizabeth Poole Design Co.; Photographer: David Sandison

14–15 (1) Architect: Simon Carnachan, Carnachan Architects; Interior design: Stewart Harris, Martin Hughes Interiors; Photographer: Michael Ng; (2) Architect: Brian Zulaikha, Paul Rolfe and Rebecca Cleaves, Tonkin Zulaikha Greer Architects; Photographer: Simon Kenny; (3) Architect: Tigerman McCurry Architects; Photographer: Leslie Schwartz

16–17 (1) Architect: Tom Catalano, Catalano Architects; Interior designer: Bierly Drake and Anthony Catalano; Photographers: Brian Vanden Brink and Sam Gray; (2) Architect: Nigel Marshall; Interior designer: Prudence Lane Design; Photographer: Anton Curley

18–19 (left) Architect: Richard Priest Architects; Photographer: Kallan MacLeod; (right) Designers: Garth Barnett, Garth Barnett Designers; Photographer: Simon Kenny

20–21 (1) Architect: Brian Brand, Baylis Architects; Photographer: Steve Keating; (2) Architect: Giles Tribe Architects and Interior Designers; Photographer: Simon Kenny; (3) Architects: Diana L. Marley and Sam Wells, Sam Wells Associates; Photographer: Tim Maloney; (4) Jane Sachs and Thomas Hut, Hut Sachs Studio; Photographer: John Umberger; (5) Architect: Darren Jessop, Jessop Townsend Architects; Photographer: Anton Curley

22–23 (1) Architect: Malcolm Taylor, Xsite Architecture; Photographer: Kallan MacLeod;

(2 & 3) Architect: Gabriel Poole, Gabriel & Elizabeth Poole Design Co.; Photographer: David Sandison

24–25 (1) Architect: Robert Weir, Weir & Phillips Architects; Photographer: David Sandison; (2) Architect: Noel Lane, Matt Brew and Mark Campbell, Noel Lane Architects; Photographer: Mark Klever

26–27 (left) Architect and interior designer: Ross Santa Maria, Impressions Pty Ltd; Photographer: Robert Frith; (right) Designers: Sandie and Daniel Biskind; Photographer: Michael Ng

28–29 (1) Interior designer: Kirsti Simpson, Bligh Voller Nield Architects; Photographer: David Sandison

30–31 (1 & 2) Architect: Paul Uhlmann; Photographer: David Sandison

32–33 (1) Architect: Trevor Abramson, Abramson Teiger Architects; Interior designer: Owners, with Elizabeth Adler Designs; Interior designer (furniture): Trevor Abramson; Photographer: Tim Maloney; (2) Architect: Brent Hulena, Hulena Co. Architects; Interior designer: Ray Lind, Martin Hughes Interiors; Photographer: Bruce Nicholson; (3) Ko Shiou Hee and Romain Destremau of K2LD Architects; Photographer: Tim Nolan

34–35 (1 & 2) Architect: Mason & Wales; Interior designer: Jewell Cassells; Photographer: Doc Ross

36–37 (1) Ko Shiou Hee and Romain Destremau of K2LD Architects; Photographer: Tim Nolan; (2) Architect: HDA Architects; Concept and interior designer: IIDA International Design; Photographer: Tim Nolan

38–39 (1 & 2) Architect: Gerard Lynch, Kevin Hayes Architects; Photographer: David Sandison; (3 & 4) Interior designer: Heather Buttrose Associates; Photographer: Tim Linkins

40–41 (1) Architect: James Gioffi; Interior designer: Donna Dunn & Associates; Photographer: Tim Maloney; (2) James McCalligan; Interior designer: James and Cherylyn McCalligan; Photographer: Tim Maloney

42–43 (left) Architect: Fery Poursoltan, Schulze Poursoltan Architects; Interior designer: Shami Griffin; Photographer: Gérald Lopez; (right) Interior designer: Margot Cordony; Photographer: Simon Kenny

44–45 (1) Designer: Vicki and Chris Seagar; Photographer: Anton Curley

46–47 (1) Interior designer: Allanah Walker Designs; Photographer: Kallan MacLeod; (2) Renovation architect: Lindley Naismith; Interior designer: Gloria Poupard-Walbridge, European Design Concepts; Photographer: Kallan MacLeod; (3) Architect: Marion Coates; Interior designer: Lorraine Rogers-Boltan, Rogers Design Group; Photographer: Tim Maloney

48–49 (1) Architect: Fery Poursoltan, Schulze Poursoltan Architects; Interior designer: Carol Hyland, Hyland House; Photographer: Anton Curley; (2) Interior designer: Margot Cordony; Photographer: Simon Kenny; (3) Renovation architect: Robert Stass, Noel Bell, Ridley Smith and Partners; Interior designer: J. & S. Myatt and Aliya Porter, Authentic Decoration; Photographer: Simon Kenny; (4) Renovation and interior designer: Devon Reid, The House of Devon; Photographer: Claude Lapeyre

50–51 (1) Architect: Fery Poursoltan, Schulze Poursoltan Architects; Interior designer: Carol Hyland, Hyland House; Photographer: Anton Curley; (2) Designer: Kerry Fyfe, Monckton

Fyfe Architects; Photographer: Simon Kenny; (3) Architect: Pat Jeffares; Interior designer and art consultant: Lenore West; Photographer: Kallan MacLeod

52–53 (1) Image courtesy of Century Furniture; (2) Renovation and interior designer: Devon Reid, The House of Devon; Photographer: Claude Lapeyre; (3) Architect: McGann-Carr; Interior designer: Brett Rogers Interior Design; Photographer: Shania Shegedyn

54–55 (left) Architect: Sandie and Daniel Biskind; Interior designer: Sandie Biskind and Jill Goatcher; Photographer: Michael Ng; (right) Architect: Jim Olson, Olson Sundberg Kundig Allen Architects; Interior designer: Terry Hunziker; Photographer: Tim Maloney

56–57 (1) Architect: Edward Niles Architect; Interior designer: Mary Beth Waterman and Steve Adams; Photographer: Kallan MacLeod

58–59 (1 & 2) Architect: Leslie Wilkinson; Interior designer: Thomas Hamel; Photographer: Simon Kenny

60–61 (1) Architect: John Durkin, Abri Architecture; Photographer: Bruce Nicholson; (2) Architect: Edward Niles Architect; Interior designer: Mary Beth Waterman and Steve Adams; Photographer: Kallan MacLeod; (3) Architect: Dan Phipps Architects; Photographer: Tim Maloney; (4) Interior designer: Jillian Friedlander, Natural Palette Colour Design; Photographer: Kallan MacLeod

62–63 (1 & 2) Interior designer: Walter Herman, Ros Palmer Interiors; Photographer: Simon Kenny

64–65 (1 & 2) Interior designer: Michael Wolk Design Associates; Photographer: Kallan MacLeod

66–67 (1 & 2) Architect: David Scott and Keith Youngman; Interior designer: David Scott; Photographer: Kallan MacLeod; (3) Deece Giles, Giles Tribe Architects and Interior Designers; Photographer: Simon Kenny;

(4) Interior designer: Neil McLachlan; Photographer: Kallan MacLeod

68–69 (left) Interior designer: Darren Grayson; Photographer: Shania Shegedyn; (right) Concept designer and interior consultant: IIDA International; Photographer: Kallan MacLeod

70–71 (1) Interior designer: Isabelle Miaja, IMA Interiors; Photographer: Peter Mealin

72–73 (1) Designer: Nigel Marshall, Marshall—The Home Creators; Interior designer: Sally Holland; Photographer: Anton Curley (2) Designer: George Budiman, Cynosure Design; Photographer: Tim Nolan; (3) John Blair, Blair + Co.; Interior designer: John Blair and Brita Corbett; Photographer: Doc Ross

74–75 (1) Architect: Andrew Patterson, Patterson Co. Partners Architects; Interior design: Owners; Photographer: Bruce Nicholson; (2) Interior designer: Gabriel Poole, Gabriel & Elizabeth Poole Design Co.; Photographer: David Sandison

76–77 Architect: Baylis Architects; Photographer: Steve Keating

78–79 (1) Architect: Sandie and Daniel Biskind; Interior designer: Sandie Biskind and Jill Goatcher; Photographer: Michael Ng; (2) Architect: John Brooks; Interior designer: Abby Smith, Egan Design; Photographer: Tim Maloney; (3) Architect: Robert Earl; Interior designer: FP Austin & Co.; Photographer: Kallan MacLeod; (4) Architect: Hut Sachs Studio; Photographer: Kallan MacLeod

80–81 (1 & 3) Interior designer: Amanda Hookham and owner; Photographer: Kallan MacLeod; (2) Renovation architect: Darren O'Neil, Architectural Studios; Photographer: Doc Ross

82–83 (1) Architect: Caroline Pidcock Architects; Interior designer: David Swan Interior Design; Photographer: Simon Kenny; (2) Architect: HDA Architects; Concept and interior designer: IIDA International Design; Photographer: Tim Nolan; (3) Designer: Glenn Holmes, Design Department; Photographer: Simon Kenny

84–85 (1) Architect: Caroline Pidcock Architects; Interior designer: David Swan Interior Design; Photographer: Simon Kenny; (2) Design: Owners; Photographer: Simon Kenny; (3) Renovation architect: Architecture Brewer Davidson; Interior designer: Melanie Stewart, Interior Design Company; Photographer: Bruce Nicholson; (4) Interior designer: Christine Baijings; Photographer: Bruce Nicholson

86–87 (left) Interior designer: Owner and Elaine Roberts—Homeworks; Photographer: Kallan MacLeod; (right) Architect: Gabriel & Elizabeth Poole Design Co.; Interior designer: Idaho Designs; Photographer: David Sandison

88–89 (1) Architect: John Durkin, Abri Architecture; Photographer: Bruce Nicholson; (2) Interior designer: Michael Wolk Design Associates; Photographer: Kallan MacLeod (3) Interior designer: Rocky Amatulli and Jenny Baron-Hay in conjunction with Craig Steere Architects; Photographer: Robert Frith

90–91 (1) Architect: Paul Uhlmann Architects with Lisa Stone; Photographer: David Sandison; (2) Architect: SCDA; Photographer: Peter Mealin; (3) Architect: Robert Blair; Photographer: Shania Shegedyn; (4) Architect: Graham Upton, Upton Architects; Photographer: Ken George

92–93 (1) Architect: Tim R. Bjella, Arteriors Architecture; Photographer: Tim Maloney; (2) Image supplied by Firth Masonry Villas

94–95 (1) Architect: Alex Gorlin Architects; Photographer: John Umberger; (2) Renovation Architect: Architecture Brewer Davidson; Interior designer: Melanie Stewart; Photographer: Bruce Nicholson; (3) Interior designer: Inscape Design; Photographer: Paul McCredie

96–97 (left) Architect: Bill Harrison and Tim Adams, Harrison Design Associates; Photographer: John Umberger; (right) Architect: Nigel Marshall; Interior designer: Prudence Lane Design; Photographer: Anton Curley

98–99 (1) Architect: Architecture Warren and Mahoney; Photographer: Lloyd Park; (2) Architect: Warren Hedgpeth, Hedgpeth Architects; Photographer: Tim Maloney

100–101 (1) Interior designer: Cathy Cowell; Photographer: David Sandison; (2) Architect: Tom Zurowski, Eastlake Studio; Photographer: Tim Maloney; (3) Main contracter and developer: YTL Development; Photographer: Gérald Lopez; (4) Architect: Eric Morrison and Pamela Rodriguez Morrison, Morrison Architects; Photographer: Mike Kaskell

102–103 (left) Interior designer: Jo Baker; Photographer: Anton Curley; (right) Architect: Patterson Co. Partners Architects; Interior designers: Neil McLauchlan and Dean Sharpe, Revolution Interiors; Photographer: Anton Curley

104–105 (1) Renovation architect: Lindley Naismith; Interior designer: Gloria Poupard-Walsbridge, European Design Concepts; Photographer: Kallan MacLeod; (2) Interior designer: Cathy Cowell, Cathy Cowell Designs; Photographer: David Sandison; (3) Architect: Guz Wilkinson Architects; Interior designer: Owners; Photographer: Luca Invernizzi Tettoni and Tim Nolan

106–107 (1) Interior designer: Suzie Beirne, Maison Jardin; Photographer: David Sandison; (2) Interior designer: Sharon Kiss, Ambiance Interiors; Photographer: John Umberger; (3) Architect: W. Allen Shumake Jr.; Interior designer: Linda Harris, The Design Shop; Photographer: Kallen MacLeod

108–109 (1) Interior designer: KA International (2) Interior designer: Peter Lloyd; Photographer: Kallen MacLeod

110–111 (left) Architect: Michael Melville, John Mills Architects; Interior designer: John Mills Architects and owner; Photographer: Paul McCredie; (right) Architect and interior designer: Craig Rossetti; Photographer: Andrew Ashton

112–113 (1) Architect: Lindy Leuschke Group Architects; Photographer: Bruce Nichelson; (2) Architect: Glasgow Architects and Robert Hanson; Interior designer: Glasgow Architects, Robert Hanson, and Maggie Bryson Interiors; Photographer: Kallen MacLeod

114–115 (1) Architect: Godward Guthrie Architects; Photographer: Kallan MacLeod; (2) Architect: Caroline Pidcock Architects; Interior designer: David Swan Interior Design; Photographer: Simon Kenny; (3) Renovation architect: Architecture Brewer Davidson; Interior designer: Melanie Stewart Interior Design Company; Photographer: Bruce Nicholson

116–117 (1) Interior designer: Thomas Hamel; Photographer: Simon Kenny; (2) Architectural and interior design: Geoff Hardy; Photographer: Simon Kenny

118–119 (1) Interior designer: Sharon Kiss, Ambiance Interiors; Photographer: John Umberger; (2) Architect: Jan Gleysteen Architects; Photographer: Kallan MacLeod; (3) Architect: Patterson Co. Partners Architects; Photographer: Bruce Nicholson

120–121 (1) Interior designer: Darren Grayson; Photographer: Shania Shegedyn; (2) Architect: Thom Craig, Modern Architecture Partners; Photographer: Kallan MacLeod

122–123 (1) Architect: Murray Wood and Jeff Karskens, Tectonic Developments; Photographer: Simon Kenny; (2) Architect: Barbara Draper, Draper Architects; Interior designer: Paul Barnett, King and Teppett; Photographer: Kallen MacLeod; (3) Architect:

Bruce Elton; Interior designer: Lucas Design; Photographer: Michael Ng

124–125 (left) Architect: Jim Olson, Olson Sundberg Kundig Allen Architects; Interior designer: Terry Hunziker; Photographer: Tim Maloney; (right) Architect: BBP Architects; Photographer: Shania Shegedyn

126–127 (1) Illustration by Heather Menzies; (2) Architect: Simon O'Brian, Six Degrees; Photographer: Shania Shegedyn; (3) Interior designer: Stanley Chong; Photographer: Bruce Nicholson; (4) Architect: Andrew Patterson, Patterson Co. Partners Architects; Interior designers: Owners; Photographer: Bruce Nicholson; (5) Photograph courtesy of L.G. Carder

128–129 (1) Illustration by Heather Menzies; (2) Architect: Gary O'Reilly and Jennifer Hill Architectural Projects; Photographer: Simon Kenny

130–131 (1) Architect: Richard Priest Architects; Photographer: Anton Curley; (2) Illustration by Heather Menzies; (3) Architect: Gabriel Poole, Gabriel & Elizabeth Poole Design Co.; Photographer: David Sandison; (4) Interior designer: Mark Peterson, M-A-Peterson Designbuild; Photographer: Tim Maloney

132–133 (left & right) Architect: Mark Singer Architects; Photographer: John Ellis

134–135 (1–3) Architect: Mark Singer Architects; Photographer: John Ellis

136–137 (1) Interior designer: Elizabeth Luke, Luke Interiors; Photographer: Simon Kenny

138–139 (1–3) Architect: Ruhl Walker Architects; Photographer: Kallan MacLeod

140–141 (1 & 2) Interior designer: Six Degrees; Photographer: Shania Shegedyn

142–143 (1 & 2) Architect: David Howell, David Howell Design; Photographer: Kallan MacLeod

144–145 (1–3) Architect: Jo Tinyou, Six Degrees; Photographer: Shania Shegedyn

146–147 (1 & 2) Architect: Novak and Middleton Architects; Photographer: Paul McCredie

148–149 (1 & 2) Renovation architect: Gregory Maire; Photographer: Mike Kaskell

150–151 (1–3) Interior designer: Owners; Photographer: Simon Kenny

152–153 (1–4) Architect: Karl de Santos, Moon Bros Inc; Interior designer: Bo Waddell, Bo Unlimited; Photographer: John Umberger

154–155 (1 & 2) Architect: Gus Wilkinson Architects; Bathroom designer: Melanie Francis, Tow Francis; Photographer: Tim Nolan

156–157 (1) Architect: Malcolm Taylor, Xsite Architecture; Photographer: Kallan MacLeod; (2) Architect: David Estreich; Interior designer: Green & Co; Photographer: Kallan MacLeod; (3) Architect: David Howell; Photographer: Andrea Brizzi; (4) Architect: Darren Jessop, Jessop Architects; Photographer: Bruce Nicholson

158–159 (left) Architect: Mark Snyder, Snyder Martung Kane Strauss Architects; Photographer: Steve Keating; (right) Architect: Joseph Paul Davis Interior Design; Photographer: Kallan MacLeod

160–161 (1–3) Architect: Joseph Paul Davis Interior Design; Photographer: Kallan MacLeod

162–163 (1–3) Architect: Florian Architects; Photographer: Mike Kaskell

164–165 (1–3) Architect: Mark Snyder, Snyder Hartung Kane Strauss Architects; Photographer: Steve Keating

166–167 Interior designer: CJ VanDaff, VanDaff Interior Design and Antiquities; Bathroom designer: Stephanie Witt; Photographer: Mike Kaskell

168–169 (1–4) Interior designer: CJ VanDaff, VanDaff Interior Design and Antiquities; Bathroom designer: Stephanie Witt; Photographer: Mike Kaskell

170–171 (1–4) Bathroom designer: Mark Cutler, Mark Cutler Design; Photographer: John Ellis

172–173 (1) Architect: Dale Mulfinger and Tim Fuller, SALA Architects; Interior designer: Talla Skogmo, Gunkelmans Interior Design; Photographer: Tim Maloney; (2) Image courtesy of Imperial Home Decor Group; (3) Interior designer: Thomas Hamel; Photographer: Simon Kenny; (4) Architect: Marion Coats; Interior designer: Lorraine Rogers-Bolton, Rogers Design; Photographer: Tim Maloney

174–175 (1 & 2) Interior designer: Elaine Roberts—Homeworks; Photographer: Kallan MacLeod

176–177 (left) Architect: Ernesto Santalla, James Solemon AIA, Studio Santalla; Photographer: Kallan MacLeod; (right) Architect: David Estreich; Interior designer: Green & Co; Photographer: Kallan MacLeod

178–179 (1–4) Architect: David Estreich; Interior designer: Green & Co; Photographer: Kallan MacLeod

180–181 (1–3) Interior designer: Jane Agnew, Agnew Interior Design; Photographer: Robert Frith

182–183 (1) Architect: Robert Middleton and Rex Bultitude, Novak & Middleton Architects; Photographer: Paul McCredie; (2 & 3) Architect: Victoria Hamer Architects; Photographer: Shania Shegedyn

184–185 (1 & 2) Architect: Ernesto Santalla, James Solemon, Studio Santalla; Photographer: Kallan MacLeod; (3 & 4) Interior designer: Margaret Goode and Karen Goode; Photographer: Steven Perry

186–187 (1 & 2) Renovation architect: Graham Pitts; Photographer: Bruce Nicholson

188–189 (1–3) Architect: Grant Amon Architects; Photographer: Shania Shegedyn

190–191 (1–3) Interior designer: Lynnda Barthlome, Elegant Interiors; Photographer: Tim Maloney

192–193 (1–3) Bathroom designer: Christine Julian, Julian Kitchen Design; Interior designer: Lynn Azeltine-Kolbusz, Room Service; Photographer: Kaskell Associates

194–195 (1) Architect: Robert Earl; Interior designer: FP Austin & Co; Photographer: Kallan MacLeod; (2) Architect: David Scott & Keith Youngman; Interior designer: David Scott; Photographer: Kallan MacLeod; (3) Architect: Ko Shiou Hee and Romain Destremau of K2LD Architects; Photographer: Tim Nolan; (4) Interior designer: Christine Baijings; Photographer: Bruce Nicholson

196–197 (1–4) Designer: Mark Peterson, M-A-Peterson Designbuild; Photographer: Kallan MacLeod

198–199 (1–3) Architect: David Estreich Architects; Interior designer: Green and Co; Photographer: Kallan MacLeod

200–201 (left & right) Designer: IIDA International; Photographer: Kallan MacLeod

202–203 (1–3) Designer: IIDA International; Photographer: Kallan MacLeod

204–205 (1 & 2) Designer: IIDA International; Photographer: Kallan MacLeod

206–207 (1) Architect: Hut Sachs Studio; Photographer: Kallan MacLeod; (2) Architect: Steven Hensel, Hensel Design Studios; Interior designer: Weinstein/Copeland; Photographer: Steve Keating

208–209 (1–3) Architect: Lindy Small, Lindy Small Architecture; Photographer: Tim Maloney

210–211 (1 & 2) Architect: Gabriel & Elizabeth Poole Design Co.; Photographer: David Sandison

212–213 (1–3) Architect: Darren Jessop, Jessop Townsend; Interior designer: Darren Jessop and Artistic Development; Photographer: Anton Curley

214–215 (1) Architect: Guz Wilkinson Architects; Interior designer: Owners; Photographer: Tim Nolan; (2) Architect: Scott Phillips and Peggy Deamer, Deamer and Phillips Architects; Photographer: Jonathon Wallen

216–217 (1) Architect: Chan Sau Yan Associates; Photographer: Peter Mealin; (2) Designer: Stanley Morris; Photographer: Peter Mealin; (3) Architect: Pavlo Szyjan; Photographer: Robert Frith

218–219 (1) Interior designer: Mark Peterson, M-A-Peterson Designbuild; Photographer: Tim Maloney; (2) Architect: Tim R. Bjella, Arteriors Architecture; Photographer: Tim Maloney; (3) Interior designer: Lyn Orloff-Wilson; Photographer: Simon Kenny

220–221 (left) Architect: David Luck; Photographer: Shania Shegedyn; (right) Architect: Lawrence Sumich; Photographer: Claude Lapeyre

222–223 (1) Designer: Sandie & Daniel Biskind; Photographer: Michael Ng; (2) Bathroom designer: Melanie Francis, Tow Francis; (3) Architect and interior designer: Renelle Jordan; Photographer: Anton Curley

224–225 (1) Architect and interior designer: Robert Weir, Weir and Phillips Architects; Photographer: David Sandison; (2) Architect: John Brooks; Interior designer: Abby Smith, Egan Design; Photographer: Tim Maloney; (3) Interior designer: Pamela Wong, Top Elegant Developments; Photographer: Bruce Nicholson; (4) Architect: Fery Poursoltan, Schulze Poursoltan Architects; Interior designer: Shami Griffin; Photographer: Gérald Lopez; (5) Interior designer: Jane

Agnew, Agnew Interior Design; Photographer: Robert Frith

226–227 (1) Architect: Butler Armsden Architects; Interior designer: Catherine Crowell Interior Design; Photographer: Russel Abraham & Tim Maloney; (2) Photograph courtesy of L.A. Carder; (3) Architect: Jane Sachs and Thomas Hut, Hut Sachs Studio; Interior designer: Joe D'Urso and Tom Flynn; Photographer: John Umberger

228–229 (1) Architect: Steven Hensel, Hensel Design Studios; Interior designer: Weinstein/Copeland; Photographer: Steve Keating; (2) Architect: Peter Lee, JPL Architectural Partnership; Photographer: Peter Mealin; (3) Architect: David Estreich Architects; Interior designer: Green and Co; Photographer: Kallan MacLeod; (4) Architect: William R. Pauli; Interior designer: Luis Ortega, Luis Ortega Design Studios; Photographer: Tim Maloney

230–231 (1) Architect: Michael Folk, Folk & Lichtman; Interior designer: Sheira Said; Photographer: Simon Kenny; (2) Designer: Peter Bromhead, Bromhead Design Associates; Photographer: Anton Curley; (3) Architect: John Brooks; Interior designer: Abby Smith, Egan Design; Photographer: Tim Maloney

232–233 (1) Designer: Darren Henault; Photographer: Andrea Brizzi; (2) Architect: Jan Gleysteen, Jan Gleysteen Architects; Photographer: Kallan MacLeod; (3) Cabinetry manufacturer: Jos van Bree, Domus Kitchens; Photographer: Shania Shegedyn; (4) Interior designer: Sharon Kiss, Ambiance Interiors; Photographer: John Umberger

234–235 (left) Interior designer: Dana Lane, Candlewick; Photographer: Shania Shegedyn; (right) Architect: Jo Tinyou, Six Degrees; Photographer: Shania Shegedyn

236–237 (1) Architect: Gabriel Poole, Gabriel & Elizabeth Poole Design Co.; Interior designer: Idaho Designs; Photographer: David Sandison; (2) Architect: Michael Wyatt; Photographer: Doc Ross; (3) Architect: Peter Ho, Graphoz Design; Interior designer: Chris and Joey Makalinao; Photographer: Tim Nolan; (4) Architect: Greg Warner, Walker Warner Architects; Photographer: Tim Maloney

238–239 (1) Architect: Edward Niles Architect; Interior designer: Mary Beth Waterman & Steve Adams; Photographer: Kallan MacLeod; (2) Architect: Hal Walters Architect; Bathroom designer: Geoff Cosier; Photographer: Shania Shegedyn

240–241 (1) Interior designer: Lyn Orloff-Wilson; Photographer: Simon Kenny; (2) Architect: Dennis Cherry Associates; Interior designer: Sheila Milano Interiors & Patricia Barash Interior Design; Photographer: John Ellis; (3) Architect: Trevor Abramson, Abramson Teiger Architects; Photographer: Tim Maloney

242–243 (left) Architect: David Luck: Photographer: Shania Shegedyn; (right) Architect: Dan Phipps Architects; Photographer: Tim Maloney

244–245 (1) Interior designer: Christine Julian, Julian Kitchen Design; Photographer: Mike Kaskell; (2) Architect: Hal Walters Architect; Bathroom designer: Geoff Cosier; Photographer: Shania Shegedyn; (3) Architect: Adam Mercer and Dick Mercer, Mercer & Mercer Architects; Photographer: Anton Curley

246–247 Architect: Jane Sachs and Thomas Hut, Hut Sachs Studios; Interior designer: Joe D'Urso and Tom Flynn; Photographer: John Umberger; (2) Architect: Gerard Lynch, Kevin Hayes Architects; Photographer: David Sandison; (3) Architect: Fery Poursoltan, Schulze Poursoltan Architects; Photographer: Gérald Lopez; (4) Architect: Gabriel Poole;

Photographer: David Sandison; (5) Architect: David Howell, David Howell Design Inc; Photographer: Kallan MacLeod

248–249 (1) Image supplied by The Ondine Electronic Shower System; (2) Designer: Mark Cutler, Mark Cutler Design; Photographer: John Ellis; (3) Architect: Jan Gleysteen, Jan Gleysteen Architects; Photographer: Kallan MacLeod

250–251 (left) Architect: Bruce Elton; Interior designer: Lucas Design; Photographer: Michael Ng; (right) Architect: Brian Brand, Baylis Architects; Photographer: Steve Keating

252–253 (1) Interior designer: Glenn Holmes, Design Department; Photographer: Simon Kenny; (2) Architect: Victoria Hamer Architects; Photographer: Shania Shegedyn; (3) Photograph courtesy of L.A. Carder; (4) Architect: Kelly Davis, SALA Architects; Interior designer: Talla Skogmo Gunkelman's Interior Design; Photographer: Tim Maloney; (5) Architect: Darren Jessop, Jessop Architects; Photographer: Bruce Nicholson

254–255 (1) Architect: Bill Harrison and Rick Hatch, Harrison Design Associates; Design consultant: Susan Botha; Photographer: John Umberger; (2) Architect: Guz Wilkinson Architects; Interior designer: Owners; Photographer: Tim Nolan; (3) Architect: Dale Mulfinger and Tim Fuller, SALA Architects; Interior designer: Talla Skogmo, Gunkelmans Interior Design; Photographer: Tim Maloney

256–257 (1) Architect: Guz Wilkinson Architects; Interior designer: Owners; Photographer: Tim Nolan; (2) Renovation architect: Graham Pitts; Photographer: Bruce Nicholson; (3) Architect: Darren Jessop, Jessop Architects; Photographer: Bruce Nicholson

258–259 (1) Architect: Caroline Pidcock Architects; Interior designer: David Swan Interior Design; Photographer: Simon Kenny;

(2) Architect: Paul Uhlmann Architects, in association with Lisa Stone; Photographer: David Sandison; (3) Architect: Michael Banney, m3architecture; Photographer: David Sandison

260–261 (left) Interior designer: Darryl Gordon Design; Photographer: Simon Kenny; (right) Interior designer: Lynn Orloff-Wilson; Photographer: Simon Kenny

262–263 (1) Cabinetry manufacturer: Jos van Bree, Domus Kitchens; Photographer: Shania Shegedyn; (2) Architect: Pavlo Szyjan; Photographer: Robert Frith; (3) Architect: Michael Folk, Folk & Lichtman; Interior designer: Sheria Said; Photographer: Simon Kenny; (4) Designer: Jennie Dunlop, Dunlop Design; Photographer: Bruce Nicholson; (5) Cabinetry manufacturer: Jos van Bree, Domus Kitchens; Photographer: Shania Shegedyn

264–265 (1) Architect: Darren Jessop, Jessop Townsend; Interior designer: Darren Jessop and Artistic Developments; Photographer: Anton Curley; (2) Architect and interior designer: Brian Zulaikha, Scott Lester, Paul Rolfe, Tonkin Zulaikha Greer; Photographer: Simon Kenny

266–267 (1) Architect: Ko Shiou Hee and Romain Destremau of K2LD Architects; Photographer: Tim Nolan; (2) Designer: Darren Henault; Photographer: Andrea Brizzi; (3) Architect: Jan Gleysteen, Jan Gleysteen Architects; Photographer: Kallan MacLeod

268–269 (1) Architect: James McCalligan; Photographer: Tim Maloney; (2) Architect: David Estreich Architects; Interior designer: Green and Co; Photographer: Kallan MacLeod; (3) Architect: Dennis Cherry Associates; Interior designer: Sheila Milano Interiors and Patricia Barash Interior Design; Photographer: John Ellis

270–271 (1) Architect: Ruhl Walker Architects Inc; Photographer: Kallan MacLeod;

(2) Designer: Mark Peterson, M-A-Peterson Designbuild; Photographer: Kallan MacLeod; (3) Architect: David Estreich Architects; Interior designer: Green and Co; Photographer: Kallen MacLeod

272–273 (1) Architect: Gerrad Hall Architects; Photographer: Bruce Nicholson; (2) Interior designer: Cheng Design; Photographer: Tim Maloney

274–275 (1) Architect: David Estreich Architects; Interior designer: Green and Co; Photographer: Kallen MacLeod; (2) Interior designer: Pamela Wong, Top Elegant Developments; Photographer: Bruce Nicholson; (3) Architect: James Roberts; Interior designer: Darryl Gordon Design; Photographer: Simon Kenny

276–277 (1) Color design: Jillian Friedlander, Natural Palette Colour Design; Photographer: Kallen MacLeod; (2) Interior designer: Suzie Beirne, Maison Jardin; Photographer: David Sandison; (3) Interior designer: Glenn Holmes, Design Department; Photographer: Simon Kenny

278–279 (1) Architect: Dan Phipps Architects; Photographer: Tim Maloney; (2) Architect: David Luck; Photographer: Shania Shegedyn; (3) Interior designer: James Young, Jacqueline and Associates; Photographer: Kallen MacLeod

280–281 (1) Architect: Gabriel Poole, Gabriel & Elizabeth Poole Design Co; Photographer: David Sandison; (2) Designer: Elizabeth Luke, Luke Interiors; Photographer: Simon

Kenny; (3 & 4) Architect: Dennis Cherry Associates; Interior designer: Sheila Milano Interiors and Patricia Barash Interior Design; Photographer: John Ellis

282–283 (1) Architect: Gabriel Poole, Gabriel & Elizabeth Poole Design Co.; Photographer: David Sandison; (2) Architect: Lisa Day, Crosson-Clarke Architects; Photographer: Anton Curley; (3) Architect: Michael Banney, m3architecture; Photographer: David Sandison

284–285 (1) Architect: Karl de Santos, Moon Bros Inc; Interior designer: Bo Waddell, Bo Unlimited; Photographer: John Umberger; (2) Architect: Richard Middleton and Rex Bultitude, Novak & Middleton Architects; Photographer: Paul McCredie; (3) Architect: Pat de Point; Interior designer: Dave Strachan; Photographer: Kim Christensen

286–287 (left) Architect: Simon Carnachan, Carnachan Architects; Photographer: Michael Ng; (right) Architect: Brent Hulena, Hulena Architects; Photographer: Anton Curley

288–289 (1) Interior designer: Sandie Biskind, Daniel Biskind and Jill Goatcher; Photographer: Michael Ng; (2) Interior designer: Mark Peterson, M-A-Peterson Designbuild; Photographer: Tim Maloney; (3) Architect: Stuart Silk, Stuart Silk Architects and Craig Stillwell; Photographer: Steve Keating

290–291 (1) Architect: Tonkin Zulaikha Greer Architects; Photographer: Simon Kenny; (2) Interior designer: Bill Cook, Vermilion

Designs; Photographer: John Umberger; (3) Architect: Mark Sheldon, GSA; Photographer: Simon Kenny

292–293 (1) Architect: Edward Niles Architect; Interior designer: Mary Beth Waterman & Steve Adams; Photographer: Kallan MacLeod; (2) Architect: James Roberts; Interior designer: Darryl Gordon Design; Photographer: Simon Kenny; (3) Architect: Richard Middleton and Rex Bultitude, Novak & Middleton Architects; Photographer: Paul McCredie

294–295 (1)Architect and interior designer: Brian Zulaikha, Scott Lester, Paul Rolfe, Tonkin Zulaikha Greer; Photographer: Simon Kenny; (2) Architect: Lionel Morrison, Morrison Seifert Murphy; Photographer: Tim Maloney

296–297 (1 & 2) Architect: Pavlo Szyjan; Photographer: Robert Frith

298–299 (1–3) Architect: Glenn Holmes, Design Department; Photographer: Simon Kenny

300–301 (1–3) Architect: Dan Phipps Architects; Photographer: Tim Maloney

302–303 (1–3) Interior designer: Glenn Holmes, Design Department; Photographer: Simon Kenny

304–305 (1–3) Architect: Denny and Svetlik Architects; Photographer: Steve Keating

306–307 (1–3) Architect: Denny and Svetlik Architects; Photographer: Steve Keating

308–309 (1 & 2) Interior designer: Jane Agnew, Agnew Interior Design; Photographer: Robert Frith